PCs made easy

STAGE 1

A PRACTICAL COURSE

Microsoft® Windows®

xp

edition

PCs made easy

STAGE 1

A PRACTICAL COURSE

Microsoft® Windows®
xp
edition

PUBLISHED BY THE READER'S DIGEST ASSOCIATION LIMITED
LONDON   NEW YORK   SYDNEY   MONTREAL

PCS MADE EASY
MICROSOFT® WINDOWS® XP EDITION
A PRACTICAL COURSE – STAGE 1

Published by the Reader's Digest Association Limited, 2002

The Reader's Digest Association Limited
11 Westferry Circus, Canary Wharf, London E14 4HE
www.readersdigest.co.uk

We are committed to both the quality of our products and the service we provide to
our customers, so please feel free to contact us on 08705 113366, or by email at
cust_service@readersdigest.co.uk
If you have any comments about the content of our books, you can
contact us at gbeditorial@readersdigest.co.uk

®Reader's Digest, The Reader's Digest and the Pegasus logo are registered trademarks
of The Reader's Digest Association Inc, of Pleasantville, New York, USA

For Reader's Digest
Project Editor: Caroline Boucher
Art Editor: Julie Bennett

Reader's Digest General Books
Editorial Director: Cortina Butler
Art Director: Nick Clark
Series Editor: Christine Noble

PCs made easy – Microsoft® Windows® XP Edition was fully updated for
Reader's Digest by De Agostini UK Ltd from *PCs made easy*, a book series created
and produced for Reader's Digest by De Agostini from material originally published
as the Partwork *Computer Success Plus*.
The new edition was adapted by Craft Plus Publishing Ltd

© 2000 De Agostini UK Ltd

Printing and binding: Printer Industria Gráfica S.A., Barcelona

ISBN 0 276 42752 1

CONTENTS

Windows®

Starting in Windows

Do you wonder how some people can make their computer work like magic? Do you want to know their secret? Well, it's probably because they know how to use Windows properly. In this section, you will learn the first steps to becoming a Windows wizard.

Without Windows your computer would be nothing but lifeless hardware. Windows operates your PC – which is why it is called an operating system.

Have you noticed how you have to wait for Windows to start before you can begin working with your computer? Once it has started, you can run other software to draw, write, play games, surf the Internet, check for email or do whatever you want to do. But

Switch on your PC and the first thing that happens is that Windows loads. Your PC can then run programs that use Windows for essential but basic tasks, such as storing your files and displaying information on screen.

Windows is always running in the background to help your other programs communicate with your hardware.

You might wonder how Windows got its name. There's a simple answer: everything in Windows takes place in its own self-contained window displayed on the screen. You can have many windows on screen at the same time and switch between them. One window might be a word processor, another a painting program or a view of files on your hard disk.

WHAT IT MEANS

OPERATING SYSTEM
An operating system is a special program that runs in the background all the time your PC is on. It handles many basic tasks such as printing and storing files on the hard disk.

UPGRADES

If you have upgraded your PC to Windows XP from another version (see pages 28–29), the XP Desktop may look slightly different to the one shown opposite – with your old Desktop icons still present and some extra buttons next to the Start button. If so, it will work in exactly the same way as before.

● You're in control

Controlling your computer is easy thanks to the graphical features of Windows. It uses icons (tiny pictures displayed on the screen) to represent different pieces of information, such as letters, pictures and programs. You use a mouse to control Windows, moving your files around, starting programs and so on. Most Windows programs use the same types of commands, which means that many new programs are easy to use because they operate with exactly the same actions and procedures. Learn the basics of Windows and you can control almost any software.

Your Desktop workspace

When you first run Windows XP, the clean and uncluttered Desktop provides as few distractions as possible. However, all of the powerful operating system features are available with a few clicks of the mouse.

Background

The background of the Desktop can be a solid colour, a pattern or even a picture. New PCs usually have either a smoothly shaded XP welcome image, an attractive landscape photo or the logo of your PC maker.

Recycle Bin

When you delete files they go here, so you can easily retrieve them if you make a mistake. To delete the files permanently, you can empty the Recycle Bin.

Desktop

Apart from the Recycle Bin icon, the initial Windows XP Desktop is empty. However, it's easy to add shortcut icons for any document, folder or other item that you use regularly, so that you can access them quickly without having to use the Start menu (see page 15).

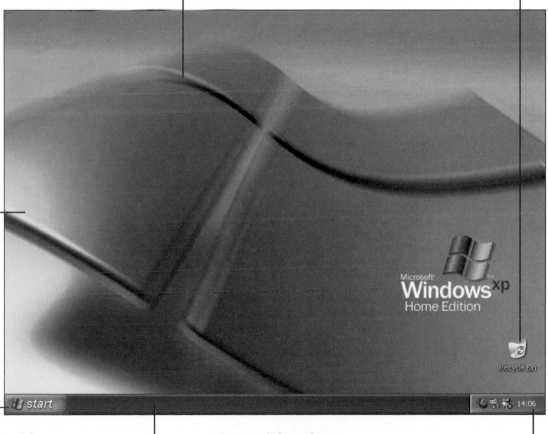

Start

This button provides the main way to access all the features of your PC. Click here and the Start menu appears; this lets you load any of the programs installed on your computer's hard drive or open any of your folders or documents. Other Start menu commands let you alter your computer's settings and get help if you encounter problems.

Taskbar

The Taskbar shows you the programs that you are currently running and the windows you have open. To switch between different windows, click on their buttons on the Taskbar.

Status/Time box

This box normally displays the current time, but it can also display other information. Pause the mouse pointer over the time for a moment and a pop-up box tells you the date. The box is also frequently used by programs to show the status of tools such as the printer, modem or battery power (on a portable computer).

Starting programs

There are several ways to start a program, but the best is by using the Start button. We shall explain how to use the Start button and look through its pop-up menus to find the programs you want to run. Here's your step-by-step guide.

THE START button is the way to reach the programs installed on your computer. You'll see this button in the bottom left-hand corner of a blue strip running along the bottom of the screen, called the Taskbar.

The Start button is a real mine of information, containing a list of all the programs and tools that are installed on your PC and storing a list of the last documents that you worked on. Later, we'll show you how to use the other tools that you can see in this menu. These include tools that provide help on any feature of Windows, search for files and set up your PC.

1 Windows' most important button is the Start button at the bottom left of your screen. Pause the mouse over the button and Windows gives you a helpful reminder of what to do.

2 Click on the Start button and a pop-up menu appears.

3 As you move your mouse around the menu, a blue bar appears on each entry. The arrowheads indicate items with sub-menus. Move the mouse over All Programs and a sub-menu appears.

4 The new list of items contains more options: folders and programs (you might have a few more or less depending on the software you have). The program we want to start is in the Accessories folder. Move the mouse over the Accessories entry and a new sub-menu appears.

5 Now move the mouse pointer down the list of items to the entry called Notepad (it also has a small picture – called an icon – that represents a shorthand notepad). Click once with the left mouse button to start the program.

6 As soon as you release the mouse button, Windows finds the Notepad program on your hard disk and starts it up, ready for you to start typing.

SHORTCUT

If you want to know more about a command or how to do something in Windows, there's always help available. Just press the [F1] key and a help screen is displayed.

PC TIPS

Tame your mouse

If you find it difficult to click on a menu option, you are probably moving the mouse too fast. Try to relax, and move the mouse slowly and smoothly. If you really cannot get to grips with the mouse, then why not cheat for the moment until you are more confident with it: click the Start button with the mouse pointer or, if you have a newer keyboard, press the Start key (in the bottom left corner between the [Ctrl] and [Alt] keys). Now use the arrow keys on the keyboard to move around the menus. Press the [Enter] key to select a menu option.

Moving and resizing windows

Let's learn how to control a Windows program. Since almost all Windows programs have the same standard set of basic commands, once you have mastered Notepad you will be in control and ready to tackle any other program.

1 If you followed the steps on the opposite page, you'll see that the Notepad program is displayed in its own window. The small flashing vertical bar (inset – called the insertion point or text cursor – shows you where your typing will appear.

2 Start by typing names and addresses of friends. As you type, the information fills the window and some moves 'off' the top – just carry on typing and Notepad will keep all your text. You can move around the text by using the up and down arrow keys on your keyboard.

3 A quick way to look around your document is to use the scroll bar. Look on the right hand side of the Notepad window and you'll see small arrowhead buttons at the top and bottom and a marker in the middle. To move one line at a time, move the mouse pointer over one of the arrow buttons and click once.

4 To move several lines at a time, you can use the mouse to drag the marker up and down the bar. Move your mouse pointer over the marker, press and hold down the left mouse button and, with the button held down, slowly move the mouse. As you move the marker, you will notice the text in the Notepad window scrolls to show you where you are. Release the button.

5 You'll often want to move the whole window to another part of the Desktop. To move the Notepad window, move the mouse pointer on to the dark blue bar at the top of the window (this is the **Title bar**). Press and hold down the left mouse button and move the mouse – you will see that the window moves as you move the mouse. Release the button when the Notepad window is in the position you want.

6 To see more of the text, you can make the window bigger. Move the pointer to the bottom edge of the window and it changes shape into a double-headed arrow. Press and hold down the left mouse button and drag the edge of the window to its new size. You can do the same to the sides of the window.

7 You'll have noticed that you can only change either the width or height of the window at one time by using the edges of the window. To change both, move the pointer to the bottom right corner of the window and you'll see it change to a diagonal arrow. Press and hold down the left mouse button and drag the window to its new shape.

8 To make the window as large as possible, use the Maximize button. Move the mouse pointer to the middle of the three small buttons in the top right corner of the window. Click once and the window will stretch to fill the whole screen.

9 Once the window is maximized, you will see that the button you just pressed looks different. If you click on the new button, the Notepad window will return to its previous size. This is known as the Restore Down button.

Switching between windows

Windows lets you run several programs at the same time, switching between them as you like. In this exercise, you'll see how to start another program – Calculator – that Windows will run at the same time as the Notepad program.

1 Calculator is a useful program that works just like a desktop calculator. Let's start this so that you have two programs running at the same time. Click on the Start button, move to All Programs, then to Accessories, then down to the Calculator entry. Click once with the left mouse button.

2 The Calculator tool will start and is displayed on the screen in its own window. Notice that another button appears on the Taskbar for this new program.

3 Depending on where your Notepad window is, you might find that the Calculator program has opened on top of the Notepad window. This often happens when you start up a new program, so being able to switch between windows and programs is an essential part of becoming a more proficient Windows user.

If Calculator has not appeared on top of Notepad, move the Calculator window by dragging it with the mouse, just as you did for Notepad in step 5 of the exercise on page 11.

4 At the moment, Calculator is active and has a slightly darker blue Title bar than Notepad. Move the mouse pointer on to any part of the Notepad window that is visible and click once. The Notepad window becomes active; its Title bar becomes darker in colour and it appears on top of Calculator.

move to page 11

A quick way to switch programs is a special keyboard shortcut. Press the [Alt] key and keep it pressed. Now press the [Tab] key. You'll see a small panel appear in the middle of the screen with icons for each of the windows you have open. Each time you press the [Tab] key you will switch to the next icon. When you have selected the icon for the program you want, just release the [Alt] key.

5 An alternative way of switching between several programs is to use the Taskbar. If you look at the Taskbar, it has the Start button, a button for Notepad and a third for Calculator. To make Calculator active again, move the pointer over the Calculator button on the Taskbar and click once with the left mouse button.

6 Notice that when a window is active – in other words, the one which appears to be on top on your computer screen – its button appears pushed in. Click on the Notepad button, and Notepad moves to the top again. This is a very effective way to switch between windows and programs when you have several open.

7 Often you will want to clear your Windows Desktop of windows and programs without actually closing them. This reduces clutter and helps you to find a particular program that is buried under a stack of other windows. Windows makes this easy; you can minimize a window – reduce it to just a button on the Taskbar, with no window on the rest of the screen – by clicking on the first of the three buttons at the top right of the window. The window shrinks to the bottom of the screen.

8 When you are working with a lot of windows open at the same time, the clutter can sometimes get in the way. If so, there's a quick way to minimize all windows so you can see the Desktop: first, click once on a blank area of the Taskbar with the right mouse button. Then select Show the Desktop from the small menu that appears.

Closing programs correctly

When you have finished using a program, you need to know how to close it. It is exactly the same with your computer. If you do not shut down either your program or computer in the correct way, you could damage your files or slow down your PC's performance.

1 Let's close down the Calculator. To close a program, move the mouse pointer to the small red X button in the top right of the window and click once. All Windows programs can be closed in this way.

2 Now move the mouse pointer to the Notepad window and close this program using the X button in the top right corner.

3 If you have not saved your work, the program will warn you and ask if you want to save it. A dialog box window pops up with three buttons:
• The Yes button lets you save your work.
• The No button lets you close Notepad and discard the work.
• The Cancel button lets you return to Notepad so you can check to see whether you need to save your work or not.

We want to save the text in our file, so click on the Yes button.

4 A new window is displayed, with the title Save As. This has several elements, but the main part of the window will list any files and folders in the My Documents folder on your hard disk drive.

5 Below this is a space where you can type in the name of the file. Let's save the names and addresses in their own file called 'My Names and Addresses' – type this into the space labelled File name.

6 Press the Save button to save the file. As soon as you press the button, Notepad stores your work on the hard disk and closes.

7 When you have finished using your computer, it is important that you shut it down correctly. When you shut down Windows, it carries out vital checks to make sure all your files are safe. If you just switch off your computer without using the correct shut down procedure, you could damage some files. To shut down Windows correctly, click on the Start button and click on Turn Off Computer at the bottom of the Start menu.

WINDOWS WARNING

Your software has lots of built-in features that help make sure you don't lose your work. Whenever you close a program, it checks to see if there have been any changes since it was last saved. Always think twice before clicking the No button – press it and all work since the last save will be lost.

8 The Turn off computer dialog box appears and the rest of the Windows screen fades to black and white. There are four buttons. Stand By adjusts the computer to a power-saving mode that doesn't turn off the computer completely – it's useful for short periods when you're not using your computer. Turn Off switches your computer off completely. Restart lets you close down Windows and reload the operating system – this is sometimes useful if Windows is behaving erratically. The smaller Cancel button is handy if you make a mistake and want to return to Windows immediately.

Click the Turn Off button and Windows closes all the files and programs that are open – including many that it uses behind the scenes. Within a few seconds your PC switches off.

Using drag and drop

Drag and drop is an essential technique that you can use in a wide range of Windows programs. Master your mouse and organize your Desktop by following these simple operations.

If you want to become an efficient Windows user, you will need to learn to control and use your mouse like an expert. Don't worry, the mouse is a friendly tool; there are just a few extra techniques to master to get the most out of Windows. Among the more useful mousing skills is a technique called 'drag and drop'.

So what is drag and drop? The phrase quite simply explains what you do: you use the mouse to select a Windows object, drag it around the screen and drop it into a new position. It's easy to learn and you'll find that you do it almost every time you use Windows. The same technique is used in many other programs.

● Drop everything

You can drag and drop all sorts of objects in Windows: for example, you can use it to move icons, files, windows and even the Taskbar. In programs there are other objects you can drag and drop, such as sections of text in word processors (Word), cells in spreadsheets (Excel) and parts of pictures in graphics programs (Paint).

● Let's do it

Before you can drag and drop an object, you first have to select it. This is simple and you've probably already done it without realizing it. Why not try it now? Go to the Windows Desktop and position the mouse pointer over the Recycle Bin icon. To select it, all you need to do is click the left mouse button. Note that the icon and the text below it are highlighted in a new colour – usually dark blue.

Now click somewhere else on the background of the Windows Desktop to de-select the Recycle Bin icon. Notice how the icon and its text label are no longer highlighted in colour.

● Change position

Let's select the Recycle Bin icon again, but this time instead of just clicking the left mouse button, press it and hold it down. We're going to use drag and drop to move the Recycle Bin icon to a different position on the Desktop.

First, let's drag it: keep the left mouse button pressed down and move your mouse as if you were using it to move the pointer. Notice how the pointer changes to a shaded image of the icon as you move it around the screen with the mouse – the original icon stays where it was.

Now for the drop: keep the mouse button pressed down and drag the Recycle Bin icon to a new position on the screen. Then, all you have to do is simply release the mouse button. This will leave the icon in its new place.

This is called dropping. Notice how the icon automatically disappears from its old position and reappears in the place where you dropped it. Dragging and dropping will soon become second nature.

Drag and drop is a Windows technique. Here's how to do it:
❶ Position the mouse.
❷ Click the left mouse button.
❸ Drag the mouse to the required position.
❹ Drop by releasing the left mouse button.

Here's a fast way to close a program, a window or Windows itself: press [Alt]+[F4]. This will close the current window. If no windows are active, it will bring up the Turn off computer dialog box.

● **Restricted areas**

There are some areas where you aren't allowed to drag and drop objects. You needn't worry, however, Windows will warn you if you are doing anything that you shouldn't – you can't break anything.

Try it. Click on the Recycle Bin icon, hold down the left button and try to drag and drop the icon on to a blank area of the Taskbar. As you drag it over the Taskbar, a restricted area symbol – a circle with a diagonal line across it – appears. If you try to drop the icon there, you'll see how Windows simply ignores your request and returns the icon to its original position.

Windows will tell you where you cannot drop items by adding a 'restricted access' symbol to the outline of the icon you are dragging.

SPECIAL SHORTCUTS

When you follow the exercise below, you'll see that the new icon on the Desktop looks just like the original (C:) icon, except for a small arrow in its bottom left corner. Windows also adds 'Shortcut to' to the original icon's text label. Try the icon and you'll find that it works just like the original. So what's the difference?

A shortcut is a pointer to the original, used to make things more convenient for you. You can add as many as you like and put them almost anywhere you like. If you delete them, the original remains safe. Many Windows users like to add Desktop shortcuts for their favourite programs to reduce the need to hunt around for them.

Dragging and dropping Windows shortcuts

Mastering this basic Windows technique will make you much more productive. In this example, we'll add a shortcut to your Windows Desktop that will give you fast access to your hard disk.

1 As you use your computer, you'll find that one window you keep returning to is the My Computer window, which contains your disk drive icons (A:, C: and D:). Usually, you'd have to select My Computer from the Start menu to get to these icons.

2 Select this command from the Start menu and its window opens to show your PC's disk drives and some other folders (don't worry about these for now). We want to add an icon for our hard disk (C:) to our Desktop.

3 Click on the (C:) icon and keep the button pressed down. The icon will be highlighted in blue. While the button is down, drag the pointer to the Desktop. Drop the icon by letting go of the button when it is in the position you want. If the My Computer window is filling the screen, click on the centre button at the top right of the bar to reduce its size.

4 Note that even though there is a new icon on your Desktop, the original remains in the My Computer window. This happens because the My Computer window is a special case – you cannot move the icons out of it.

5 You can also add icons for your floppy disk and CD-ROM drives, and for items in the left-hand panel. Just repeat steps 3 to 4. If you want to move an icon once it is on the Desktop, you can just drag and drop it as necessary.

Introducing the Clipboard

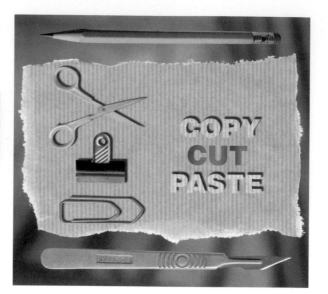

The Clipboard is one of Windows' best features; it makes copying words, numbers and pictures between documents easy. Here's how to use the Clipboard's built-in intelligence to get more out of Windows.

As you work with Windows programs, you'll find you often need to move information from one part of a document to another. Perhaps you need to duplicate the same words several times, or maybe you need to copy most of the text from one letter to a different letter.

The good news is that Windows has a special feature that makes all of this easy. Forget laborious retyping – with a few simple commands the Clipboard can do it all. It can even copy pictures or tables of numbers.

● What is the Clipboard?
The Clipboard is a special area of your PC's memory that can hold a temporary copy of any information you like. You first choose the information you want to copy, and then get Windows to copy it to the Clipboard. Then you choose where you want it to

go and get Windows to paste it from the Clipboard to the new position.

● Select to copy
The key to letting Windows know what you want to copy is to ensure that you select it. You can try this right now in Windows' simple word processor program, WordPad.

In WordPad, type a few sentences. Choose some words that you wish to copy to another part of the page. Put the mouse pointer just in front of the word, press and hold the left mouse button, drag the mouse to the end of the word and release the button.

Take note that as you drag the mouse, the text you have selected changes from black letters on white to white letters on blue (see right). Then you need to copy it to the Clipboard. Click on the Edit menu, then click on the Copy command from the drop-down list that appears. It looks like nothing has happened, but Clipboard now has a copy of your word.

● Paste the word
Choose where you want the word to go. Put the mouse pointer at the required position and click once. The words you originally selected revert to black text on a white background, and the insertion point moves to the new position. Click on the Edit menu, then click on the Paste command in the drop-down list. The copied text appears at the indicated location in the document.

Cutting, copying and pasting with the Windows Clipboard takes the drudgery out of repetitive documents.

Copying from program to program

On the opposite page you saw how to cut, copy and paste text in WordPad. Now let's see how easy it is to use the Clipboard in an especially useful way: to copy information from one program to another.

1 Start WordPad and Calculator (they're both in the Accessories folder in the All Programs sub-menu of the Start menu).

Move and resize the WordPad window until the two programs are side by side as shown here. If you're not sure how to move and resize a window, refer back to the exercise on page 11.

2 Copy this sample letter in WordPad. To complete the letter, you'll need to work out how much the payments will come to.

All you have to do is move the mouse pointer to the Calculator window, click somewhere on it to make it active and then you can work out the calculation.

3 You can either click the mouse on Calculator's buttons or use the keyboard's numerical keypad. (Make sure the [NumLock] key is pressed and its light on the keyboard is lit before you try to use these keys.) Enter the following calculation: '99.95*36='
The Calculator display will give you the exact answer as soon as you click the [=] button.

4 Now you know the answer, you could just retype the answer into WordPad, but that presents the risk of a typing mistake. Instead, we'll use the Windows Clipboard to store the answer.

Click on Calculator's Edit menu (inset) and click on Copy from the drop-down list. Note: in this particular case, you don't even need to select the answer before copying.

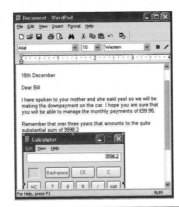

5 Switch to the WordPad window by clicking inside it, and position the insertion point at the appropriate position by clicking the I-beam pointer just to the right of the last line in the WordPad window.

Click on the word Edit in the menu bar and click Paste from the drop-down command list. An exact copy of the answer to the calculation is copied into your WordPad document.

6 Many programs accept other types of information from the Clipboard. Switch to the Calculator and press [Alt]+[PrintScreen]. This copies a picture of the Calculator to the Clipboard. Go back to WordPad and position the insertion point at the end of the document.

7 Now use the same Edit and Paste commands from WordPad's menus as you did in step 5. The Windows Clipboard knows that WordPad can handle pictures just as well as text, and it pastes a picture of the Calculator window into the document at the position of the cursor. This is a very useful trick we'll look at in detail later in the course. (Note: you can change the size of the picture by clicking and dragging any of the eight square 'handles' on the edges of the picture.)

Save the letter into the My Documents folder, following the steps on page 13.

PC TIPS

The right mouse button

Your mouse can help when cutting and pasting. Instead of moving the pointer to the Edit menu, you can select the text you wish to move, then click the right mouse button.

This pops up a menu of options, including Cut, Copy and Paste, which you can use in exactly the same way as the Edit menu options.

Understanding files and folders

Your computer's hard disk can store thousands of letters, pictures and programs. All these files can easily clutter up a system, so to keep it all organized and manageable, Windows uses folders. Here's an explanation of how files and folders work.

A computer is like an electronic office, and your data and work is stored in Windows much the same as papers are stored in an office. Just as an office has hundreds of documents, and therefore requires a filing system, so your computer also needs a filing system to keep track of all your work.

The key to understanding how your computer manages files – which can be programs, letters, pictures and so on – is to compare it to the way documents in an office are stored. You'll see there are plenty of similarities; the only real differences are because your computer is much more flexible and powerful than office filing systems.

If you share your PC with your family, it's important to make sure everyone understands the basic principles concerning files and folders on your hard disk.

● Documents, files and folders

An ordinary office has many types of document, from single page letters and photographs to multi-page reports. It's usual – and often essential – to keep related documents together in a folder. These folders might also be stored within other objects, such as a filing cabinet, for example.

Your computer works in just the same way. The basic unit for storing computer information is a file. This is exactly equivalent to the office document: photographs, letters, reports and so on (programs on your PC are also stored as files).

● Don't worry about size

Windows also lets you keep related files together in folders – just like the office. The big difference is that you don't have to worry about the physical size of your documents and folders. Putting a three-inch thick report into a one-inch thick folder is impossible in

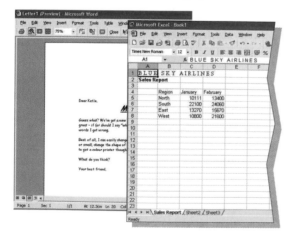

Every time you save a letter, spreadsheet or other document, you create a file on your hard disk. Windows lets you store these files in electronic folders so that you can avoid disorganized clutter.

WHAT IT MEANS

EXTENSIONS

The extension is part of the file name added at the end. You'll often see .txt, .bmp, .doc and .xls and there are many others. Windows uses the extension to remind itself which program to use when working on a document.

real life, but Windows will let you put huge files into a folder. This electronic folder will happily swallow whatever you put in it. You can also put folders in folders – almost impossible in real-life.

Just as every office worker makes sure files and folders are labelled with a name or number for easy storage and retrieval, Windows makes sure that files have names: 'letter to gran', for instance. Depending on how your PC is set up, you may also see three letters tacked on to the end of a file's name. These are called extensions and let Windows know what type of file it is. A .doc extension would be for a Word document, for instance.

● Disks and filing cabinets

All your files and folders are stored on disks in your computer (floppy disk, hard disk and CD-ROM). The only real limitation on the number of documents such disks can contain is the amount of space the files take up. Rather like a storeroom in an office, a disk starts off empty, but can become jam-packed over time with programs, letters and other documents (see pages 98–99).

In the step-by-step guide below, you can see how the folders and files stored on your computer appear through Windows. On page 21, we show you how to create and use your own folders.

Exploring files and folders on your hard disk

Find out how files and folders work by browsing through your hard disk.

1 Let's start your exploration of your files and folders by clicking on the My Computer command on the Start menu.

2 You'll see a new window which shows icons for the disk drives in your PC together with a collection of other icons. Double-click on the (C:) icon, which represents your hard disk.

3 The window that pops open shows the files and folders stored on your hard disk (the exact number and type depends on how many you have created and the software you have). Folders look like miniature versions of the manilla folders you'll find in every office (above right). Files look like miniature pictures of various types of documents (left).

4 Double-click on the Program Files folder to see what's inside. You'll see something like this: a collection of files folders (they are called sub-folders) for the programs installed on your computer. Just browse through these sub-folders for the moment – don't click on any of the files inside the folders. Use the toolbar's Back and Up buttons to retrace your steps. Close the window by clicking on the X button at its top-right corner.

PC TIPS

As you browse through folders on your hard disk, you will often find that some windows are so full of icons that you can't find the file or folder you're looking for. If this is the case, you can use the window's View menu (inset) to change the way the contents appear. Click on View and then click on Details in the menu. The window will change to show a list of items in the folder. This listing makes better use of the window by shrinking the icons down and you also get to see more details for the items, including file size and type. The list is in alphabetical order, so it's very easy to read down the list until you find the item you're interested in.

There are two ways to store your work: the messy way, where you can never find anything, and the organized way. Organize your computer now and you'll save time in the long term.

Managing files and folders

You can save your files anywhere on your hard disk, but if you want to be able to find them again easily, it is best to use the tools provided in Windows to create folders and organize your files logically. This is a more efficient way to work that will save you a lot of time and avoid unnecessary problems.

It is possible to save all of the documents that you write, graphics that you design and spreadsheets that you create in your My Documents folder. However, while keeping everything together in one folder is better than haphazard filing, it's not ideal. For instance, once you have stored masses of files in just one folder, it becomes hard to browse and find a particular document.

● Organized chaos

Think about how you organize your paperwork and documents at home or work. You don't just pile them all in one place. Ideally, you group them by subject headings and store them in separate folders with easy-to-remember names.

This is also the best way to store your files in Windows. As you'll see in the step-by-step guide opposite, it's simple to create a folder for any subject you're working on and save the relevant files in it. Unlike real folders, computer folders are free, too!

After a while, you may find these new folders become cluttered with lots of files, but don't worry – you can always create sub-folders within your main folder and move files from one folder to another any time you like.

● Folders make life easier

Once you've created your folders, you can move them around your hard disk as easily as any type of file. A big advantage of this is that when you want to move a folder – perhaps to make a copy on a floppy disk – all the files and folders inside it will be copied, too.

Just as there seems to be no end to the number of Russian dolls that can fit inside each other, you can continue to put files and folders into other folders on your hard disk as many times as you like.

PC TIPS

A shortcut to the *PCs made easy* folder

Once you have created the *PCs made easy* folder on your hard disk (see opposite), you can create a Desktop shortcut to it. That way you don't need to do so much double-clicking through lots of other folders to find it.

To do this, use the right mouse button to drag the folder from the window onto the Desktop. A small menu pops up to ask what you want to do with the folder: click on Create Shortcuts Here. A new icon for the folder will appear on your Desktop.

> Copy Here
> Move Here
> Create Shortcuts Here
> Cancel

Creating and using a new folder

Here's how to create your own *PCs made easy* folder on your hard disk. Once it is created, you can start organizing your documents by copying and moving files you have already saved on your hard disk.

1 To start, click on the My Computer command in the Start menu. When the My Computer window opens, double-click on the (C:) drive, which represents your hard disk.

2 Your hard disk contains lots of files and folders. To create a new folder, move your cursor to the left-hand panel and in the second pane under File and Folder Tasks, click on Make a new folder.

3 The new folder is simply called New Folder, but you can type over this label with the name you want the folder to have. In this case, type in *PCs made easy* and press the [Enter] key.

4 Double-click on the new *PCs made easy* folder to open its window and repeat steps 2 and 3 to create a new folder inside it. This time name it Word.

5 Now you can move one of the files you have created into your new folder. Click on the Start menu and open the My Documents folder from the My Computer window. Move the My Documents and *PCs made easy* windows until they are side by side. Click on one of the files: we've chosen a Word document called 'acceptance letter.doc' – use one of the files you have already saved.

6 Drag the file icon from the My Documents window to the Word folder in the *PCs made easy* window. As the mouse pointer moves over the yellow Word folder, note that the folder becomes highlighted to show that is where the file will go when you drop it. Drop the icon on the folder.

7 Notice that the original icon for the file you have moved disappears from the My Documents window. That is because Windows made an intelligent guess that because you dragged the file icon to a place on the same disk, you wanted to move it and not copy it. Most of the time this is correct, but sometimes you will want to keep the original in the same place.

8 Copying a file, rather than moving it, is a simple matter of pressing the [Ctrl] key during the drag-and-drop operation. Try it now with one of the other documents from your My Documents window. The icon you are dragging with the mouse pointer has a small + sign next to it to indicate that the file being dragged is 'in addition' to the original. Drop the icon on the Word folder and the original stays in place.

Directories and paths

Learning to find your way around the numerous folders on your hard drive is a useful skill. Once you understand the logical structure, you will never have trouble finding a file again.

On pages 18–21, you looked at the concept of folders, which form the basic building blocks for storing your files and documents on your PC. However, you might have wondered how these files and folders are stored on your hard disk and how they are organized. To know this you need to understand the concepts behind directories and paths.

● Branching out

The structure of the many different files and folders on your hard disk is often called a directory tree. The analogy of a tree, with its roots and branches, is quite a useful one. The root of the tree is equivalent to the **root directory**, the most basic level of your hard disk.

Just as a tree has branches, so your hard disk has folders, or directories. And as the branches of a tree can split into many more branches, so the directories on your hard disk can branch off into further directories. These branches are not pre-determined when you buy your computer – you create them as you install software, or make folders in which to store your own files and documents. There are very few limitations on how you develop your directories – you can create as many levels as you need.

● Descriptive path

Most of the time you navigate your way around the hard disk by double-clicking on folder icons. Sometimes, however, it's better to describe the location of a file or folder as a simple line of text which indicates the route, or 'path', to the file/folder as it branches off from the root. It will help you to understand this more fully if you go through the step-by-step exercise opposite.

Understanding how files and folders end up where they do on your hard disk will help you manage your computer more effectively and efficiently.

WHAT IT MEANS

ROOT DIRECTORY

The root directory is the top level of folder on your hard disk – within which all other folders are stored – and from which everything on your computer 'grows'. Its path is very simple: just the letter of your hard drive followed by a colon and a backslash, such as 'C:\'.

*Image labels:*

C:\PCs made easy\Mum's stuff\Savings.doc

C:\PCs made easy\Mum's stuff

C:\PCs made easy

C:\

Following the file path

When you understand just a little about paths and directories it will be easier both to store and find files on your computer.

1 Click on the Start menu and select the My Computer command. You'll see the usual collection of hardware devices and special folders, in addition to the disk drives on your computer. Double-click on the hard disk icon (usually labelled [C:]) to see the contents of the root directory.

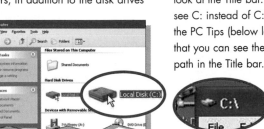

2 When the new window appears, look at the Title bar. If you see C: instead of C:\, use the PC Tips (below left) so that you can see the full path in the Title bar.

3 Choose one of the folders and double-click on it. When the folder window opens to reveal its contents, you'll see that the path in its Title bar is different.

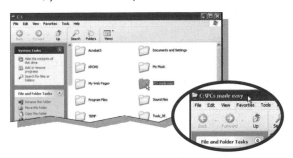

PC TIPS

If you want to know the path of folders as you navigate through them, there is an option in Windows to display the full path in the Title bar of any folder. To do so, go to the Tools menu and choose Folder Options. Click on the View tab and click with the mouse to put a tick next to the option called Display the full path in title bar.

4 Double-click on a folder within this new window (if necessary, you can create one – see pages 20-21). If you look at the path of the window that appears, you can see that it uses a backslash [\] character to indicate different levels of directory.

5 Use the right mouse button to drag any of the files from this folder to the Windows Desktop. Select the Create Shortcuts Here option when Windows asks you what you want to do.

6 Right-click on the new shortcut for your document and select the Properties option from the drop-down menu that appears.

7 Click on the Shortcut tab of the dialog box (right) and you'll see that the Target text box shows you the exact path of your document file. The full path includes the disk drive (C:), the route through the folders you double-clicked on (\PCs made easy\Word) and the name of the file, which in our example is acceptance letter.doc.

Windows programs use paths to keep track of the files and folders they are working with. In addition, paths are used by Windows to locate and start programs.

TARGETS AND PATHS

When you create a shortcut you are telling Windows to go to a specific place on your hard drive. This place is called a Target and Windows creates a path to it. Windows uses the Target when you double-click on a shortcut. The Target retraces the path through the folders to find and start the program or open the document.

Windows Explorer

Most of the time, it's easy to open the My Computer window and then click on the objects and folders within it to look through the files and folders stored on your computer. However, if you find that the Desktop gets cluttered when you've got several windows open, take a look at Windows Explorer which brings them all together in a single window.

By now, you should be experienced at opening and using the My Computer window to explore your PC and look at the files, folders and other objects stored on your hard disk, floppy disk and CD-ROM drives. This window contains large icons that represent your computer's hard disk, the floppy disk drive, the CD-ROM drive and other icons that allow you to view the documents stored on your computer.

● Inside your computer

If you're interested in seeing what files and folders are stored on your hard disk, all you have to do is double-click on the large icon that represents the hard disk; it's usually called (C:). Then Windows will open a new window that shows icons for the top level of files and folders stored on the hard disk. If you want to examine the contents of a particular folder, all you have to do is double-click on its icon and Windows will open another window that contains icons for each file and sub-folder within that folder.

This simple-to-understand technique has only one real drawback: your Desktop can soon get cluttered if you open lots of windows. You often have to move the various windows around on screen to see the contents of the folders you're interested in. However, Windows includes another tool that you can

use to view your files and folders. This other tool avoids unwanted clutter: it's called Windows Explorer.

To see how Explorer works, click on the Start button in the Windows Taskbar and choose All Programs and then Accessories. Now choose the Windows Explorer option from the menu that appears; you'll see that the icon beside it looks like a magnifying glass over a folder.

● Explorer panes

The Windows Explorer window is split into two parts, usually referred to as panes. The left pane contains icons for all the main parts of your computer, such as the Desktop, hard disk drive, floppy disk drive and CD-ROM drive. Click once on the hard disk icon (C:) in the left pane, and the right pane fills up with icons for the top-level files and folders on your hard disk.

Double-click on one of these folders and the contents of the right pane will change to show the contents of that folder. You'll notice how, at the same time, the left pane changes to show a tree view of the hard disk: you can see all the folders it contains.

As we'll see in the exercises on the next three pages, Windows Explorer is quite a powerful way of exploring your computer in a single window.

WHAT IT MEANS

TREE VIEW

This describes the hierarchical view of the disks, files and folders stored on the PC. Windows Explorer represents your PC as a tree of objects stored inside other objects. Each part of your PC (for example, the hard disk) is a branch. Every folder within one of these branches is treated as a sub-branch and so on down to individual files.

A tree view of your computer

To keep tabs on a huge collection of loose documents, folders and objects, Windows files all your contents hierarchically.

THE TREE VIEW used in Windows Explorer views the Desktop as the top level of the hierarchy of your PC, with everything else as an element on the Desktop. For example, My Computer, which represents the hardware components of your PC, is treated as an item on the Desktop.

The next level below this in the hierarchy contains components that can store data such as files, folders and other objects. This also includes items such as your hard disk, floppy disk and CD-ROM drives.

Below this, each component that can store data has its own, separate, hierarchical structure of folders that can contain files and sub-folders which, in turn, can contain more files and sub-folders. Organizing your files and using simple names makes items easier to find.

Even though the words 'hierarchical structure' and 'top level view' may sound like computer jargon, they make sense when you see a graphical representation of the way your files and folders are organized by Windows.

You can see in this diagram how the hierarchy works. My Computer is the top level (in reality, the Windows Desktop is the top level), and below this is the tree-like structure of files and folders. At the next level down are the three icons that represent the floppy disk, hard disk and CD-ROM drives. Assuming we don't have a floppy or CD-ROM disk inserted, we continue down the hierarchy through the hard disk drive and see a 'branch' of five folders. We follow the hierarchy through the PCs made easy folder, where we see folders for Excel and Word files and a Paint file (Map1.bmp).

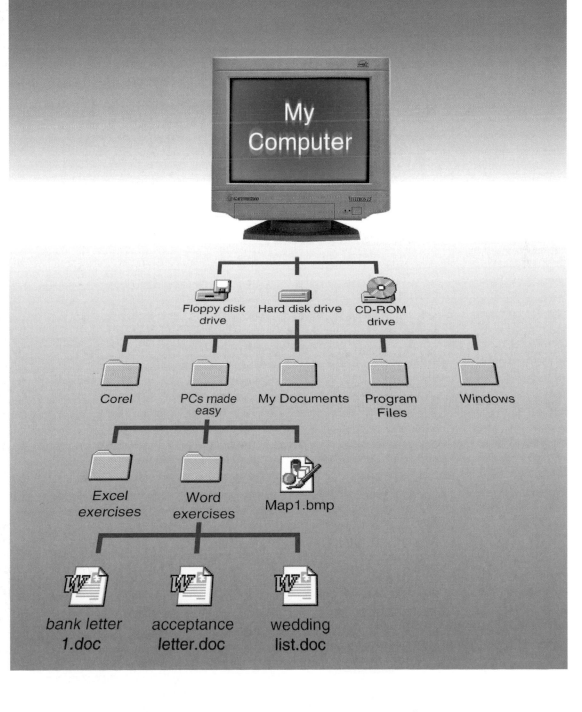

Viewing files and folders with Explorer

Use a handy shortcut in Windows Explorer to see how the items on your computer are related to each other.

1 Click once on the Start button and wait for the menu to appear. When it does, right-click on the My Computer command and select Explore from the pop-up menu.

2 Notice how the Windows Explorer window is split into two panes. The left pane shows the top-level parts of your computer (such as the hard disk). When you first open Explorer, this structure is duplicated in the right pane. Now click once on the hard disk icon in the left pane.

3 The right pane changes to show lots of icons – one for each object stored at the next level down in the hierarchy of your hard disk. Double-click on the Program Files folder in the right pane.

4 The right pane will change to show icons for all the files and folders held in the Program Files folder. Don't worry if your computer shows different folders to those shown here – the exact contents of this folder depend on the software installed on your PC. You must be careful not to move or delete anything within the Program Files folder.

5 Exploring without making changes is fine, however. Double-click on one of the folders. The right pane shows the contents of this folder and the left pane shows the next level down of the tree structure. Notice how this folder's icon in the left pane is open as a reminder.

6 So that's how you move down the tree structure in Windows Explorer, but how do you get back up? That's just as easy: all you have to do is click on the Up button (inset) in the toolbar at the top of the Explorer window.

PC TIPS

Opening folders quickly

If you work through the exercise on this page, you might notice that little plus and minus signs keep appearing and disappearing beside the folder icons in the left pane of Explorer. When a plus sign appears beside a folder, it means that the folder contains sub-folders. The quick way to see these sub-folders is to click on the plus sign. Explorer will then show them in the left pane as the next level of the tree view.

When you do this, the plus sign changes to a minus sign. Click on the minus sign to close the folder. This technique also works for icons that represent other types of objects in Explorer, such as the Desktop itself, the hard disk and the CD-ROM drive.

Choosing different views

If you're happy with the large icons that you usually see in the My Computer window, you can get Windows Explorer to show information about files in the same way.

THERE ARE obvious differences between the way things look and behave when you use Windows Explorer, compared to the look of files and folders in the method we've seen before when using the My Computer window. For a start, everything happens in one window with a tree view when you use Explorer, as opposed to a separate window for each folder when you use the My Computer window. These are just two ways of looking at the same information.

Here is how you can alter the right pane of the Windows Explorer view; the left pane always shows the tree view with small icons.

1 Windows Explorer has a toolbar that gives you ways to alter its appearance with a single click. If the toolbar isn't visible when you start Explorer, go to the View menu, click Toolbars and select Standard Buttons from the sub-menu.

2 The Views button on the far right of the toolbar gives you control over Explorer's appearance. The selected view option here is List, which shows a simple list of files, folders and other objects in the right pane with small icons beside them.

3 If you want to see more information about each object in the right pane, you'll need to select the Details option. To do this, click the Views button and select Details.

4 The right panel changes to show extra columns of information. You can explore your files and folders in this view, or try another.

5 Windows Explorer can show items in the right pane as large icons, too. Select Tiles using the Views button. The downside of the Tiles view is that they take up a lot of space. Try the Icons option if this is a problem.

Upgrading to Windows XP

If you want to update your PC to the latest version of Windows, you must check your hardware and software for compatibility with Windows XP before you start.

I f you're currently using Windows 98 or Me, you can change to the latest version of Windows, XP, by buying and installing the upgrade package. Many of the everyday computing techniques and procedures are similar for all versions of Windows, but Windows XP has some major new developments.

In addition to a fresh look and feel, there are improvements in functionality. Both the Start button and the Taskbar work differently, making it faster and easier to get at your programs and to open documents than before. Folder windows have a new panel down the left-hand side which is full of useful options. These change as you work giving you short cuts to save time when carrying out common tasks.

UPGRADING FROM WINDOWS 3.1 & 95

The Upgrade version of Windows XP only works with Windows 98 and Me. If you use an earlier version, such as 3.1 or 95, you must buy the Full version. Because the full version does a fresh install, it's imperative that you do a full backup of your documents so that you can copy them back to the hard disk after installation.

● New face, similar personality

However, most of these aspects simply enhance the way that previous versions of Windows worked, so you don't have to abandon the knowledge you've already built up. Instead, you can use Windows XP just like your old OS, exploring the new options as you come across them. The look and feel of Windows XP is also just as easy to change as your old OS. You can change the colours, background images and many other aspects. You can even revert to the Windows 95/98/Me look, which is now called the Classic view.

● Under the surface

Many previous versions of Windows for home users were based on MS-DOS, with Windows running on top as the user interface. Windows XP, however, does not use MS-DOS as the basis for its operating system. Breaking free of the limitations imposed by MS-DOS has enabled Microsoft to make Windows XP work more efficiently in many areas and eliminate the need for two separate OSs. The two versions of Windows XP – Home Edition and Professional Edition – are essentially identical, except for office-orientated networking and minor details in the Professional Edition.

● More reliable

For home users, the new OS means that Windows XP is a lot more reliable than previous versions. The chances of a program crashing and freezing Windows, thereby requiring you to restart the PC, are much reduced with Windows XP.

The Home Edition of Windows XP is the version for the home user. Anyone upgrading from 98 or Me will find it familiar in its layout and actions, but will benefit from its extra reliability and security.

WINDOWS XP COMPATIBILITY

Before you upgrade to Windows XP you must first check your software is compatible. Some programs written for earlier versions of Windows may not run at all on Windows XP. If you have Windows XP on your PC, you should ideally buy only software with a Windows XP logo; other programs may need an upgrade. At the beginning of any installation, Windows XP checks to make sure that the programs are written to a new Windows XP compatibility which ensures that installing them cannot harm the Windows XP OS itself.

Some Windows 98/Me software will work fine, but check the software company's Web site or ask your computer retailer for advice on using it on Windows XP before buying.

Upgrading to Windows XP

If you want the benefits of Windows XP you can upgrade from earlier versions of Windows, but it pays to do some research first.

AS WITH ANY new operating system (OS), the vital question for PC users is 'Is it worth upgrading?' The answer in many cases is 'Yes', but you need to make sure that your PC is up to the task before splashing out.

Windows XP places high demands on your PC's hardware. Microsoft's recommendations are a 300MHz or faster processor, 128MB of RAM and 1.5GB of hard disk space. Of these demands, it is most likely that you

will need more RAM (see pages 100-101). Memory is inexpensive, so this will only cost about £20.

If you have added hardware to your PC, be aware that some drivers may be incompatible with Windows XP. This OS is significantly different to Windows 98 and Me, and a few devices that work perfectly with those OSs may not work after upgrading. All is not lost, however, as almost all hardware manufacturers are adding

drivers for Windows XP to the download areas of their Web sites.

As part of the setup process, XP will report any software or hardware that needs updating. You can update during installation or wait until later.

The upgrade process itself is straightforward, and takes an hour or so, plus any download time. As with any OS upgrade, make sure your documents are properly backed up before you start.

1 Installing Windows XP is easy, but if your PC has lots of hardware add-ons and a mixture of software programs, it's worth checking their compatibility before you start. Select the first option to get Windows XP to check your PC automatically.

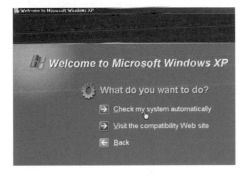

2 Follow the on-screen instructions; the new OS takes about an hour to install, and it provides feedback on progress through the various stages on the left of the screen.

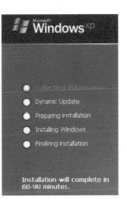

3 Windows XP will report any hardware or software that may be problematic; you can click on Full details to get information and suggested solutions.

4 The Windows XP setup program suggests downloading the latest setup files from its Web site, but you can select the option to check these later to avoid increasing the installation time with a lengthy download.

5 After installation, the Windows XP Desktop appears. On a new PC, the Windows XP Desktop lacks most of the icons that earlier versions of Windows used such as My Computer and My Documents. However, depending on your PC and the options you selected during the installation process, these icons may be present. As you use Windows XP it will automatically suggest removing any of these icons that you don't use to decrease Desktop clutter.

PRODUCT ACTIVATION

One of the most important changes in Windows XP is product activation. This is Microsoft's method of countering software piracy. When you install Windows XP you are given 30 days to activate it; if you don't, Windows XP stops working.

To activate it, click once on the keys icon that appears near the clock at the far right of the Taskbar. Follow the prompts in the window that appears. You can activate Windows online or by telephone. In either case, your PC is assigned a unique code – no-one else can activate another copy of Windows using your Windows XP CD-ROM.

Software

Microsoft®Paint

Success with words

Word processing – creating text documents on a computer – is the most frequently performed task on a PC. In PCs made easy, we take you step-by-step through one of the top programs in the field, Microsoft Word.

W ord processing is the term used to describe all the activities associated with creating text documents on a computer. This covers letters, curriculum vitae, reports and memos, flyers and school or office projects; in fact, almost any form of written document. The beauty of word processing is that once you have typed your document, you can save it, alter the look of it using the many tools built into each program, and print out as many copies as you need.

● **Improving features**

Microsoft Word is one of the most popular word processing programs on the market. The program has been around for a long time, but it is constantly being improved and updated with new features. Don't worry if you have a slightly different version of Microsoft Word to the one shown on the opposite page, or even if you have another program, such as WordPerfect. It might have slightly different

menus or toolbars, but the same basic principles of word processing still apply.

● **First words**

With a word processor, you can correct any mistakes you make before you print your document, move around a document quickly using your mouse, delete and reposition individual words or blocks of text, and even check your spelling. To alter the appearance of your finished document, you can change the margins and format of your pages. You can make some of the text bold, italic or even put it all into a different typeface. The list of features goes on and the possibilities are huge. The more you use a word processor, the more you will realize its potential.

The first thing to learn in Microsoft Word is where all these tools and functions are located. On the following pages, we shall guide you through the process of opening a blank page in Word, and taking the initial steps towards creating your first letter.

THE [ENTER] KEY

This is the large key just to the right of the main set of letter keys, next to the square bracket [ ] keys. It's also known as the [Return] key. This key is also repeated at the bottom right of the numeric keypad.

Making a start on a blank page

It's now time to start Microsoft Word from Windows and introduce you to all the main features of the word processing program. Have your mouse at the ready.

TO BEGIN working on a Word document you first have to start the program. This is simple. Switch on your computer and monitor, and wait until Windows appears.

Using your mouse, put the pointer on the Start menu in the left corner of the screen and click with the left button. A pop-up menu will appear. From the list, choose All Programs. When the second menu appears, click on Microsoft Word. The Word start-up screen will appear, followed automatically by a blank page. This is your first document, called 'Document1'. The words and buttons you can see are the tools with which you control the program.

Menu bar
The nine subjects on this bar each give access to a pull-down menu. Simply click on a word to reveal the list of commands under each subject.

Toolbar
Toolbars are very useful and feature icon buttons that allow you to give the program commands without having to go through the pull-down menus. This section contains the most commonly used command buttons, such as the ones that open and close documents, print, check the spelling and cut and paste the text.

The icons in this section of the Toolbar alter font (typeface) type and size, make highlighted text bold, italic or underline it, create indents and generally help you shape the look of your document. Microsoft Word has many toolbars, which you can hide or display, depending on the task you want to perform.

Title bar
The line of text at the top of the screen that shows the program you are using (Microsoft Word) and the name of your file ('Document1').

Toolbar options
The default format shows the Standard and Formatting toolbars together on one line. The width of your window will determine how many of the icons will fit onto your toolbar. To access the additional options, click on the small black downward pointing arrow at the end of each toolbar section. This will also give you the option of whether you would like these two main toolbars displayed on one line or separately on two lines.

Ask A Question box
To get quick guidance on using Word, you can type in a question here and press the [Enter] key.

Task Pane
Windows XP has this additional panel which provides shortcuts to common functions. To show or hide the Task Pane and provide more room to work on your document, click once on the X next to the title of the Task Pane. To show the Task Pane, click on View in the Menu bar and select Task Pane from the drop-down menu. We will deal with this in more detail later in the course.

Insertion point
A flashing vertical line that appears on the page to show where any text you type will be inserted.

Status bar
The bar at the bottom of the screen that shows further information about the document on which you are working, such as which page you are on.

Ruler
This is below the Toolbar and can be used to alter tabs and margins on a typed document.

Scroll bars
Beige horizontal and vertical bars at the bottom and right-hand side of a document allow you to scroll through a page. There are three types of scrolling: click on the black arrows to move the page up or down, and left or right; or click on the beige scroll boxes within the bars, hold the left mouse button down, and drag the boxes along the bars; or click within the bars themselves and move the page in stages.

Laying out a letter

Creating documents in Microsoft Word couldn't be easier – follow these simple steps to produce your first word-processed letter.

THERE ARE times when a neatly typed letter is much more appropriate than a hand-written one, particularly in business or formal correspondence. The same applies to your CV and job applications, reports, projects and many other documents.

The great thing about word processing programs is that you can start using them straightaway. All you have to do to enter text in Word is start typing. Later in the course, we will delve deeper into editing techniques such as copying and moving text, and changing the look of the words to make them stand out, but for the moment we'll keep it simple.

● Start typing

As discussed earlier, the flashing vertical line – called the text cursor or insertion point – indicates where the next character you type will appear. As you type, the insertion point moves horizontally towards the right of the screen. Unlike a typewriter, you do not have to press [Enter] every time you come to the end of a line, because the word processor automatically moves to the next line. If you

wish to separate paragraphs of text or begin a sentence on a new line, simply press the [Enter] key and the insertion point will move down a line.

● Your first letter – step 1

Try this exercise to create your first document. Start by copying the text from step 1 (below). Type it exactly as we have, pressing the [Enter] key when you want to move on to the next line. Don't worry if you make a mistake, press the [Backspace] key to remove the mistake and retype the word.

● Moving text with tabs – step 2

Now that you have completed the exercise of typing in the text, we shall show you the most simple method of converting it into letter format, as shown in step 2 (on the opposite page). When setting out a letter, it is conventional to put your own address and the date of writing on the right-hand side of the page. Rather than adding lots of spaces to move your text along the line, it is better to use the [Tab] key.

Tabs are useful if you want to create paragraph indents, align your text in columns or put measured spaces between words. To insert tabs, click the insertion point in front of the word or sentence you want to move, then press the [Tab] key. Word pre-sets

Word-processed documents are preferable to hand-written letters when entering into formal correspondence, such as applying for a new job.

[TAB] KEY

The [Tab] key is just to the left of the [Q] key. Some keyboards use an arrow and line symbol, others are printed with 'Tab'.

S H O R T C U T S

To move the insertion point around your document, you can use a set of special keys, called cursor keys. They allow you to move the insertion point to any position on any line. The arrow on each key shows the direction that the insertion point will move when you press it.

Moves the insertion point up one line

Moves the insertion point forward one position

Moves the insertion point back one position

Moves the insertion point down one line

1 Copy the letter exactly as we have typed it. When you need to start a new line, simply press the [Enter] key.

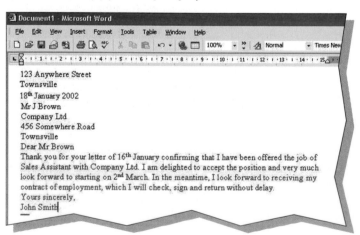

123 Anywhere Street
Townsville
18th January 2002
Mr J Brown
Company Ltd
456 Somewhere Road
Townsville
Dear Mr Brown
Thank you for your letter of 16th January confirming that I have been offered the job of Sales Assistant with Company Ltd. I am delighted to accept the position and very much look forward to starting on 2nd March. In the meantime, I look forward to receiving my contract of employment, which I will check, sign and return without delay.
Yours sincerely,
John Smith

2 To format the letter, click in front of the text you want to move. In this case, it is the sender's address. Press the [Tab] key until the address and date align on the right-hand side of the page.

3 To make a blank line, all you need to do is press the [Enter] key at the beginning of an existing line.

4 After you've finished your letter, you should save it. Click on the File menu, and then click on the Save As option from the drop-down menu list.

5 You'll see a Save As dialog box. Type a name for your letter and click on the Save button.

its tabs so that the text is moved along 13mm (½ inch) at a time. Later in the course, we'll show you how to set tabs just where you want them.

Keep pressing the [Tab] key until the longest line of text has moved as far to the right as it can without any of it dropping on to the next line. If you press [Tab] too many times and the text moves on to another line, simply click in front of the text and press the [Backspace] key to delete as many tabs as necessary until the whole line fits.

● Inserting blank lines – step 3

Once you have tabbed the sender's address across to the right-hand side of the page, click the insertion point just in front of the date. We want to insert a blank line between the address and the date. To do this, press the [Enter] key. This moves the text down a line. Then use the [Tab] key to move the date along until it lines up below the address.

The recipient's name and address conventionally stay on the left-hand side of the page, so insert a line space to separate it from the date. To do this, click the insertion point in front of the recipient's name (Mr J Brown) and press the [Enter] key again.

Follow the same procedure to insert line spaces between paragraphs until your document looks just like the one in step 3. Use several blank lines to give enough space to sign the letter. When you have finished, you are ready to print.

When you print out the letter, you will see that Word has added a margin to all sides of the page, so the text doesn't start quite as close to the edge of the paper as it looks on the screen. Later in the course, we'll show you how to change the margins to suit different documents.

● Saving – steps 4 & 5

After you've finished typing your letter, you should save it. Click on the File menu, and then click on the Save As option. The screen that pops up – a dialog box – lets you give your letter a name. Type the name and then click the Save button. To close the Word window, click on the File menu and click Exit.

**S H O R T
C U T S**

Many of the commands in Windows programs can be completed without using the pull-down menus. Most programs have quick commands that can be activated via the keyboard. Try the following shortcuts using only your control key [Ctrl] plus the letter indicated:

Create new document
 [Ctrl]+N
Open document
 [Ctrl]+O
Close document
 [Ctrl]+W
Save document
 [Ctrl]+S
Print document
 [Ctrl]+P

Liven up your letters

Make your letters stand out from the crowd by adding extra flourish to your words. Here's how to use Word's Formatting options to jazz up your documents with the press of a few buttons.

For many of us, letter writing is the main reason – and possibly the only time – we put words on a page. It is also the type of writing that can call for very different approaches to style.

Some types of letter – such as the job acceptance letter in the exercise on pages 34–35 – need a formal approach. You can format others in a much more informal and fun way – such as personal letters to friends and members of your family.

● Friendly formatting

One of the great things about Microsoft Word is that whatever style of letter you want to create, you use exactly the same formatting features to achieve them. There are two main groups of formatting tools: firstly, text formatting tools that change the appearance of text, and secondly, page formatting tools that alter the overall look of the pages. Depending on the toolbar setup you are using (see page 33), you may find these toolbars are set out differently but they contain the same tools.

In this exercise, we shall concentrate on how you can make your letters look attractive with the text formatting tools.

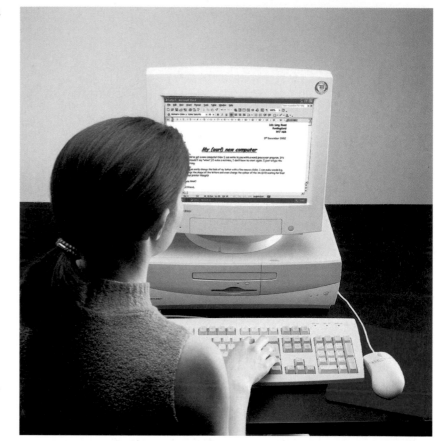

The Formatting options on the toolbar

Word's toolbars give you access to many powerful commands with a single click of the mouse. Here's a guide to the most useful buttons. Use them to change the look of the text in your letters and documents.

Styles and formatting	Typeface	Text size	Text weight	Alignment	Others
To quickly change the appearance of specific characteristics of text using pre-defined style sheets.	Use this drop-down list to select a typeface for your text. Click on the down arrow on the right-hand side and a list will drop down to show your choices. Scroll down this list to see more typefaces.	Use this drop-down list to select the text size. Click on the downward pointing arrow and choose the size you want. You can also change the number by clicking on it and typing a new number.	You use these buttons to select the emphasis of the text. The B makes text bold, the I makes it italic and the U underlines it. To turn off any of these effects, just click on the button again.	These buttons align text. Look closely and you'll see they show the effect they have, aligning text left, centre, right or justified (on both sides). These buttons affect whole paragraphs, not just the selected text.	We'll tackle the other buttons later. With them you can create special lists, change text and background colours (very useful if you have a colour printer) and add borders and frames.

Adding a touch of style

Word has tools and commands to turn your plain letters into stylish and personalized documents that get you noticed. Here's a step-by-step guide to text formatting.

1 The first thing to do is to open a new document and type the text of your letter. For this exercise, use the text shown here (and in step 8), or use a letter you've already created.

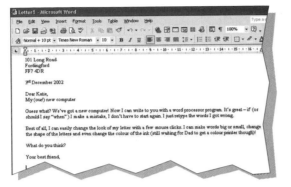

2 Let's move the address and date to the right-hand side of the page. First, select the address and date by dragging the mouse pointer from the first letter of the first line down to the last letter of the date. Now click on the Align Right button on the toolbar. If you're unsure which is which, pause with the mouse pointer over each button and Word will tell you with a small yellow label.

3 Let's use the same set of buttons to centre the title of the letter. Click once anywhere in the title line and then click on the Center button on the toolbar. Notice that you don't have to select the whole line.

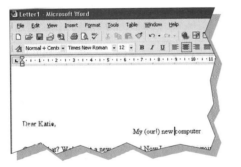

4 We want to change the **font** used in the letter to a more fun one. To select all the text, click once on Edit in the Menu bar and then click on Select All from the list of commands.

5 All the text changes to white on black, and now you can change the formatting of the whole document at once. To change the font, click once on the typeface list box and scroll down until you see Comic Sans MS (you might have different fonts on your computer depending on your software).

Click on the font you want and you'll see the whole letter change. Experiment with different fonts and see how they change the look of the letter.

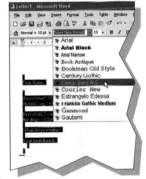

6 To change the emphasis of the letter's title, select it (by dragging the mouse from the first letter of the title to the last) and click on the Bold, Italic and Underline tools. You could also make the address bold.

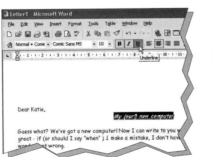

7 To make the title stand out even more, change the size of the text. With the title selected, click once on the font size list. When the list appears, select a size of about 18 (the letters will be about 6mm [one quarter of an inch] tall).

8 Here's our final letter. Remember that we chose fonts and styles to add a fun appearance to our letter. You can also use exactly the same commands to choose different fonts and sizes to make letters more business-like. Experiment with some of your letters.

101 Long Road
Fordingford
FF7 4DR

3rd December 2002

Dear Katie,

My (our!) new computer

Guess what? We've got a new computer! Now I can write to you with a word processor program. It's great – if (or should I say "when") I make a mistake, I don't have to start again. I just retype the words I got wrong.

Best of all, I can easily change the look of my letter with a few mouse clicks. I can make words big or small, change the shape of the letters and even change the colour of the ink (still waiting for Dad to get a colour printer though)!

What do you think?

Your best friend,

WHAT IT MEANS

FONT
This is printing jargon for typeface, the overall design of letters and numbers. Look at this page of PCs made easy and you can see several typefaces: most of the text is in a font called Futura Book, the headlines are Futura Condensed Bold, while this text is Sabon Italic.

Mastering templates

Many of the documents we create, including letters and invoices, are variations on a theme. They contain many common elements: layout, formatting and often whole chunks of text. Templates save you time and trouble by storing this standard information in a form you can modify again and again.

A template is a re-usable document containing information that you will use repeatedly in your work. For example, it might be an invoice template in which you have entered all your relevant details, such as a VAT number, bank account, company name and address, and so on. So, rather than starting from scratch each time you want to make an invoice, you simply open an existing template, changing or adding only the necessary details.

You will find that templates are invaluable for all sorts of word-processed documents. Even everyday letters benefit: instead of typing your name and address and the date each time you write a letter, you can use a template to add these automatically. This leaves you free to concentrate on getting the main body of the letter right.

Templates can also minimize the chances of making embarrassing typing mistakes: once your template contains the correct information, you can be sure that every document you create based on the template will definitely include exactly the same words. The time spent checking that the information contained in your templates is correct will be time well spent!

● Filling in the blanks

Other types of document are also best created as templates for you to fill in the blanks. If you create lots of faxes, for example, which all need boxes for the recipient's name, sender, fax number and date, a template will boost your efficiency.

Templates can include anything you can put into a Word document. If you want a template with special formatting, for example, you can create one with the same typeface and type size changes that you used in the exercise on

There are several useful templates stored ready for use with Word. This is a résumé (curriculum vitae) template – you need only replace the information with your own.

SHORT CUTS

Often in Word, you will want to select all the text in your document to make a change to it – changing the typeface (font) and its size, for example. Instead of using the Edit menu's Select All command, you can use a keyboard shortcut instead: press [Ctrl]+[A]. You'll immediately see the whole document become highlighted, changing from black text on white to white text on black.

Microsoft® Word

WHAT IT MEANS

READ-ONLY

Windows can set a file so that you can read it but you can't write any new information to it. This is called a read-only file. If you open a read-only document, you can edit it and add words to it, but you must use the Save As menu option instead of the Save option. This ensures you save a new file and the original remains intact.

page 37. On pages 46–49 we'll show you how to add simple pictures to your documents and templates. In the exercise below, you'll also see that Word has ready-made templates that include lines, boxes and multiple columns. Documents such as fax header pages often incorporate such layout techniques.

● Template names

Template names always end in '.dot', so that you can distinguish them from normal Word documents. Because a template is intended to serve as a model for similar documents, Word does not allow you to alter it by saving it in the normal way. These files are **read-only** documents. When you use a Word template as the basis for a new document, you can only save it as a '.doc' file. The original template remains unaltered.

PC TIPS

If you often add lists of items or objects to your documents, try Word's automatic bullet point button (right) to create them. It's easy to use and creates a properly formatted list

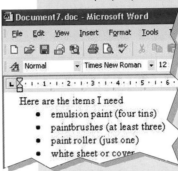

with indents (left). Just select the lines of text you want made into a list, and click once on the button. Word will do it all in an instant. (Note: the button just to the left of the Bullets button produces a numbered list.)

Opening a template in Word

Word's ready-made templates help you get a head-start in creating attractive documents. Here's how to do it.

1 Start Word and open the Task Pane (see page 33). If the Task Pane heading is not New Document, click once on the arrow next to the X and select it. Go to New from template and click on the General Templates link.

2 The Templates dialog box appears. Move the mouse pointer along to the tab labelled Letters & Faxes, and click once to see the ready-made templates available in this category.

3 Click once with the left mouse button on the 'Contemporary Fax' template. You will see a preview of the template appear automatically on the right side of the dialog box.

4 While the small preview helps you get an idea of the template and its style, there's no substitute for looking at it full size. Click the OK button to load a new document based on the template into Word for editing.

5 Notice that this fax template contains all the normal fax headings such as 'To:' and 'From:' and dummy text for you to replace. There is also a high level of formatting, with text at different sizes and in various typefaces.

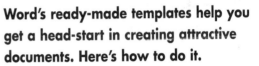

6 Experiment with the template – change some of the text, and then click on Save from the File menu. Notice that the Save As dialog box appears and Word has suggested 'Contemporary Fax.doc' as the file name – the original 'Contemporary Fax.dot' remains unchanged as templates are read-only files.

Creating a new template

If you can't find a suitable template from those supplied with Word, you can create your own from scratch. It's as easy as creating a normal document, and the Task Pane means you can find it in a trice.

1 Let's create a new template using Word's Task Pane. Look in the list under New Document, then New from template. Click once on the General Templates link. (If the Task Pane heading is not New Documents, click once on the arrow next to the X to select it.)

2 In the Templates dialog box that appears, click on the General tab and select Blank Document. At the bottom of the right-hand panel, under Create New, ensure that the Template option has a black dot in the white circle by clicking once on it. Then click on the OK button.

3 You now have a blank template document open on screen. To start, just type in your name and address. Then select these lines of text. The Align Left button is automatically selected. Click on the Align Right button (inset) on the toolbar to move it to the right side of the page. (We have turned off the Task Pane to use the whole screen area for typing.)

4 Now change the font for the name and address part of your letterhead: with the text selected use the drop-down Font menu to choose a new font. Scroll down to find one you like, and then click on it once.

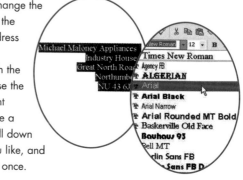

5 Change the size of your address text by using the drop-down font size list. Try sizes between 14 and 20. Do experiment – try choosing fonts and sizes that give your letterhead different types of character: businesslike, informal, etc.

6 To insert the date without having to type it in by hand, choose Date and Time from the Insert menu (inset). A small dialog box pops up that lets you select the date and time format. Word can supply many different formats at the click of a mouse button. Use the scroll bar to move through them, then click once on the one you want. Above the OK button, you'll notice a small check box, labelled Update automatically. If there is no tick in this box, click once on it to make one appear. Then click on the OK button to return to the template.

8 Today's date now appears in your document, at the position of the text insertion point. Every time you use this template to create a new document, Word will insert the correct date. Like all other parts of your template, you can also change the appearance of the date – font, size, etc. – just using the normal menu options and tools. The documents you create from this template will reflect this.

9 Now add a subject line to the document. Press the [Enter] key three times to create some space after the date line. Then type in a subject. If you find you often create letters with the same subjects, you can make a template for each to save more time when you write the letters. Remember to name them appropriately so that you use the right one.

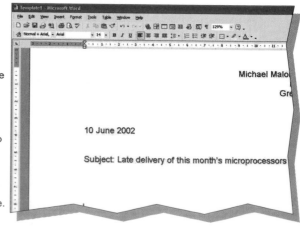

10 Centre the subject line by selecting the line and clicking once on the Center button on the toolbar.

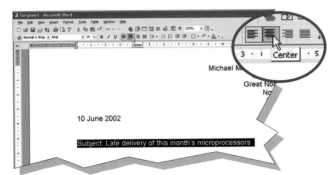

11 With the line still selected, click the B button on the toolbar to make the subject bold. The line will change from plain to bold text.

12 All that remains is to add a salutation and a sign-off. Underneath the subject line, insert a blank line then a 'Dear Sir or Madam' line. If it appears centred in your document, use the Align Left button to correct it.

13 Leave a few blank lines under the salutation – this is where you'll add the main body of your letters when you use the template. Now type a closing, including your name with space for a signature.

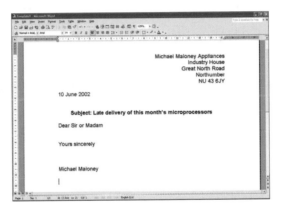

14 Now it's time to save your letterhead template for future use. Move the mouse pointer to the File menu, click once and then click on the Save As option.

GREYED-OUT MENU ITEMS

As you use the menus and options in Word, you'll often come across menus and options that you can read, but not select. These entries have light (greyed-out) text instead of the usual black.

The greyed-out menu items indicate operations that cannot be performed at the current time. In this case (below), we've just started Word straight after starting Windows. Before typing anything, we've clicked on the Edit menu.

Notice that most of the options are greyed-out. Think about them for a moment and you can see how this makes sense. You cannot Copy or Cut anything from the document because there is

nothing selected. Likewise, you cannot Paste anything into the document because there's nothing in the Clipboard (Windows has just started, so the Clipboard is empty).

15 A dialog box appears, and Word suggests a name based on the first line of text in the template. If you don't want to use this name, simply delete Word's suggestion using the [Backspace] key and type in your title. Make sure that Document Template appears in the Save as type box at the bottom of the dialog box. Click on Save.

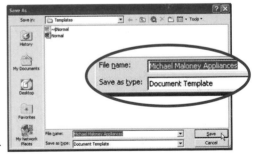

16 Now when you open the General Templates option you'll see your new template listed. Click once on this icon and then in Create New click on Document, then OK.

17 A new document will open, ready for you to fill in the blanks. You can go straight to the main body of your letter and type in the important parts, confident that the other parts are exactly as you entered them into the template. Notice that the date also changes to show today's date.

How to work faster with Word

Whether you are working with long documents or lots of short letters, Word has several tricks up its sleeve to help you get through your work more efficiently. Here's how to boost your speed skills.

Most PC users spend a lot of their time using their word processor. Because it's the most popular piece of software, the software's programmers have added many shortcuts and special tools to help you make more effective use of your time.

Here, we'll cover some of the tricks in Word's repertoire that you might not have spotted yet, which can help you work faster and smarter in Word.

● Cut, copy and paste
We've already seen how the Cut, Copy and Paste commands found in the Edit menu are extremely useful tools (see pages 16–17). For Word users, it gets even better – Word can use drag and drop (see pages 14–15) to move parts of your document as quickly as you can use the mouse.

These techniques are probably the most effective skills a Word user can have. See the box below for a step-by-step guide.

● Page control and previewing
We shall also introduce some powerful ways in which to manage how your documents look on paper. And we'll show you how to avoid guesswork when it comes to printing.

Word processors have many built-in features – activated by your keyboard and mouse – which can help you complete routine tasks more quickly.

COPY AND PASTE VERSUS DRAG AND DROP

Copying and pasting in Word work much like they do in other Windows programs (see pages 16–17). You select the words or paragraphs you want to copy or move, copy them into the Windows Clipboard and paste them in the new position.

Select some text in your letter or document, click on Edit in the Menu bar and click on the Copy command from the drop-down list.

Move the text insertion point to the position you'd like the copied text to go and then select the Paste command from the Edit menu.

Alternatively, you can use the drag and drop technique we covered on pages 14–15 to copy and move text in Word. As with all drag and drop techniques, you start by highlighting the text you want to copy. This lets Word know what text you want to move.

Once your text is highlighted, move the mouse pointer over it and click and hold down the left mouse button. Now move the mouse down; you will see the pointer change to show a special symbol (a rectangle, right), which indicates that Word has 'picked up' the selected text.

Move the pointer to the position where you want to place the text and let go of the mouse button. The text moves as soon as you release it.

Starting on a new page

As you type, Word will add a page break when you fill each page. For more precise control over the appearance of your documents, you can also add your own breaks.

WHAT IT MEANS

MARGINS

Margins are the white spaces that surround the printed area of the documents you create in Word and other programs. By default (automatically), you will get a white border of 2.5cm (about an inch) on each of the four sides of your pages. We'll show you how to change the size of these margins later in the course.

IF YOU HAVE typed long documents in Word, you will have noticed that every so often the program automatically inserts a dotted line right across the Word window. You will probably also have noticed that when you print your documents there is no such dotted line across the page.

In fact, the dotted line appears exactly at the position where one page finishes and another starts. The dotted line is there to show you when you've reached the bottom of a page. It is Word's visual reminder of the boundary between pages, called a page break.

If you experiment by adding lines of text to a page, you'll notice that the dotted line moves. Word automatically calculates the number of lines you can have on a page. This figure depends on the paper size, the margins and the size of your text.

● Automatic or manual?

The trouble with Word's automatic page breaks is that sometimes you will want to deliberately start a new page – for example, to begin a new chapter or section of a document. So how can you insert a page break exactly where you want it?

Word gives you the power to do this by inserting a manual page break, a code that tells Word that no matter how many text lines there are on the current page, you would like the next line to start on a new page.

Like automatic page breaks, the manual page break appears as a dotted line across the window, but with the words 'Page Break' to show it's a fixed page break. If you want to remove a manual page break, you just delete it. Put the text insertion point on the line and press the [Delete] key on your keyboard.

Inserting a manual page break

You don't have to accept the page breaks Word automatically gives you, nor do you have to insert lots of blank lines just to move on to the next page. Here's how to be in full control of your page breaks.

1 To insert a manual page break at any position in the document, first move the text insertion point to the position you want the new page to start (you can use the mouse or the cursor keys to do this).

Click on the Insert menu and then click on Break from the list of commands.

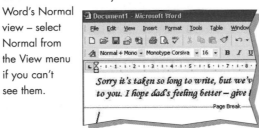

SHORT CUTS

There's a quick way to insert a page break straight from the keyboard. If you press [Ctrl]+[Enter] you will see a dotted page break line appear at the position of the text insertion point.

2 The Break dialog box pops up in the middle of your Word window. Make sure Page break is selected (it should have a black dot in the small white circle; if it doesn't, click on the circle once). Click on the OK button to return to your document.

3 After the dialog box closes, you will see a dotted line across the document with the words 'Page Break' centred in it. This serves to remind you that this break is one that you have created rather than an automatic one added by Word. Therse lines are used in Word's Normal view – select Normal from the View menu if you can't see them.

4 New text appears right after the dotted line – it will be the first thing printed on that page. This is very useful for creating pages where you need only a small amount of text at the top of each page. It's much better than adding lots of blank lines to push text on to new pages.

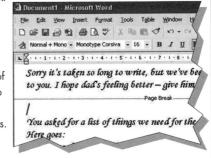

Previewing before printing

It's not always easy to visualize how your document will look when you print it. So here's how you can get Word to let you check your document before you print pages you may not be happy with.

WHEN YOU take a lot of effort to prepare a lengthy word-processed document, it's all too easy to lose sight of how it will actually look when you print it out on paper. If you print the document without checking it, you could end up wasting a lot of time redoing

Print Layout view lets you see how each page of your document would look when printed and allows you to edit it directly.

something because it doesn't quite look as you expected it to.

To avoid this pitfall, Word provides a print preview tool. This shows you on the screen what your document will look like on paper without you having to actually print it.

Use Word's print preview feature to check that your letters and documents look right before committing them to paper.

● Saving paper

If you can get into the habit of using the preview before you print each document, you'll save yourself lots of paper. In particular, it's very useful for catching those instances when a single line carries over from one page on to another. When you catch this problem through the preview, you can go back to the document and correct it before printing.

You can get to the print preview tool by selecting Print Preview from the File menu (top, right). When you do this, all the normal toolbars at the top of the Word window will be replaced by just one toolbar and the main editing area of the screen will display a picture of the whole current page (above).

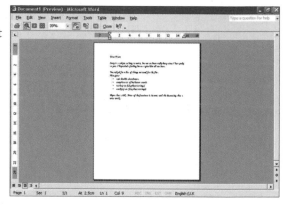

You'll notice that the mouse pointer changes to a small magnifying glass with a '+' sign inside it (right). This indicates that you can click to zoom in and see a close-up view. Once you have zoomed in, the pointer changes to show a '–' sign; click with this pointer and you'll zoom back out again.

● Page by page

If your document has several pages, Word will display the page you were working on when you chose Print Preview. Use the [Page Down] and [Page Up] keys (or use the scroll bars) to move from page to page to see the rest of the document.

If you spot a problem, click the Close button on the toolbar to go back to your document and make any changes. Of course, once you're happy with what you see in the print preview, you can print your document by clicking on the Print button at the far left of the toolbar.

PC TIPS

At the bottom of Word's right scroll bar, you will see these three small buttons. The two double-arrowhead buttons work like page turners – quickly moving to the top of the page before or after the one you are currently working on. The middle button is used for moving between different objects in a document. We'll show you how to get the most from this button later in the course.

Scrolling around your documents

The longer your Word document becomes, the more difficult it is to find your way around it. Here are our tips for hassle-free document navigation.

MOST DOCUMENTS are too big to fit on the screen all at once. Scrolling is the basic Windows technique you can use to move backwards and forwards through a document so that its other parts are displayed on screen. The easiest way to scroll through a Word document is to use the scroll bar down the right side of the window.

All you have to do is press the button at the bottom of the scroll bar with a down arrow on it to move forward through your document. If you want to move backwards, press the button at the top of the scroll bar with an up arrow on it.

There is another scroll bar along the bottom of the Word window so that you can move sideways in wide documents.

● **Drag and drop scrolling**
The alternative is to drag and drop the slider button inside the scroll bar. This has the added advantage that Word tells you where you are in the document through the pop-up yellow page number box (see below).

Practise scrolling – it's a lot quicker than using the cursor keys to move through a document one line at a time. You'll also find that it is a useful technique in Windows.

Two views on one document

Sometimes it is useful to be able to look at two different parts of the same document. If scrolling back and forth is too tiresome, here's the tip that solves the problem.

1 Move the mouse pointer to the thin button right at the top of the scroll bar (inset). You will see it change from the usual pointer shape to a special double-headed arrow. The arrows indicate which directions you can drag the button.

2 Click on the scroll bar button, then, keeping the left mouse button pressed, drag it down the screen. As you do, you'll see that the pointer drags a thick grey line down through your document. Drop the line halfway down your screen.

3 As soon as you drop the line, you'll see that the button expands horizontally to become a divider that fits across the Word window. This divider splits the single Word window into two independent panes, each with its own scroll bars.

4 To work with two views on the same document, just use the scroll bars so that each pane shows one of the areas that you are interested in. Drag the scroll bar with the mouse as usual (the small yellow page indicator can help you locate particular pages on your longer documents, inset).

When you no longer require two panes to view your document, simply drag the divider bar back up to the top of the scroll bar. When you let go, it will revert to its small, thin-button state on the right-hand side.

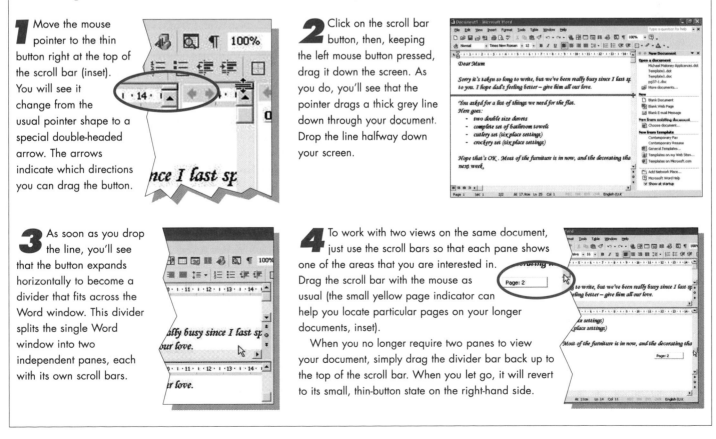

Adding pictures and special effects to documents

They say that a picture paints a thousand words, so it's good to know that Word lets you insert pictures to liven up your letters. Here's our guide to spicing up your documents.

So far we've used Word for the bread-and-butter job of manipulating text. However, the most interesting documents use special effects and pictures to liven up plain text that might otherwise look boring.

Word has the tools to help you create a thrilling party invitation just as easily as you can write a sober business letter. But it isn't just fun documents that benefit from jazzing up – pictures and text effects can help reinforce the serious messages you might want to convey in your business documents.

● More ways to add style
We've already seen how altering text size, emphasis and typeface can change the appearance of your letters. Now we'll see that Word has another trick up its sleeve for really exciting text effects: the WordArt tool.

You can use WordArt to type in any word or phrase and then stretch and squeeze it in many more ways than you can with normal text. For example, you can rotate WordArt text to any angle, give its letters outlines in one colour and fill their insides with a different one, or distort text by changing its height and width. You can also decide how the normal text in your document will **wrap** around the special text objects you create with WordArt. You can even choose to make the text run along curves and wavy lines. WordArt is an easy tool to master and you can create some really stunning effects with just a little practice and experimentation.

Stretch your words to any shape you want with WordArt.

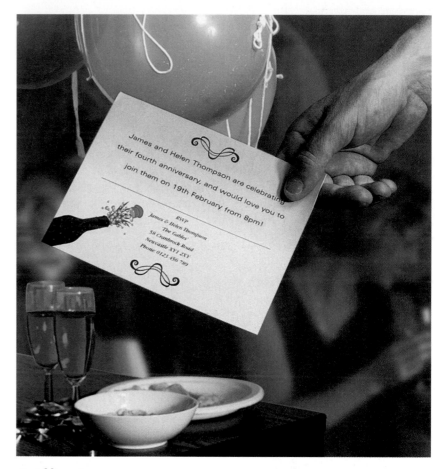

● Adding pictures
Word also gives you a simple way to add pictures to your documents and letters. You can use pictures supplied as part of the Word software package, or graphics you have created in Microsoft Paint or another graphics program. Adding photographs is equally easy.

As with the text in WordArt, once you've inserted a picture you can manipulate it in many ways. For instance, you can move the picture in the document, change its size and distort its shape. You can also decide how the text in your document will wrap around the picture, and you can change the colours in it by altering brightness and contrast.

There's no reason why you need to put up with lifeless text-only letters. Add some sparkle to your documents with the following step-by-step guides.

Many documents are much more attractive when you add pictures and special effects.

WHAT IT MEANS

WRAP
Place an object into your document, and text runs – or wraps – around it. Photos usually have a square (or regular) wrap. The hands stretching the balloon on this page look better with a wrap that follows their shape (irregular wrap).

Using WordArt to create a party invitation

WordArt is an easy and fun way to be more creative with your PC. If plain text just won't do for your documents, here's how to give them a new lease of life.

1 Let's see how you can use Word's WordArt tool to create special text effects to liven up a party invitation. First, you'll need to type in and format the text for your invitation. Here we've typed the main part of the text in 12pt Times New Roman with some text aligned left and some aligned right.

2 To create a piece of WordArt, click on the Insert menu, click on the Picture option from the drop-down list of commands and then click on WordArt (inset).

3 The dialog box you now see (below, left) shows simple previews of the WordArt styles available. There are plenty to choose from; choose an appropriate one and click on the OK button. Now you'll see the dialog box where you can type in your text (below, right). Simply type a phrase such as 'Come To My Party!', choose 40pt as the size and select a typeface from the list box – we've picked Impact. When you click on the OK button, WordArt will apply the style of your choice to the words you've typed in.

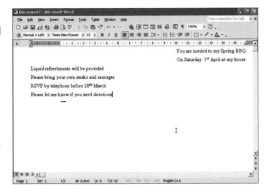

4 You will see the text appear in your document. Click the WordArt text and the floating toolbar will appear.

We want our text to wrap around the WordArt object. Use the Text Wrapping button on the WordArt toolbar to select Top and Bottom. Green, white and yellow handles will now appear at regular points around the text.

5 Use the white circles to resize the text, and the yellow diamond circles to change the waviness of the text. The green circles allow you to rotate the angle of the text – experiment to see how they work.

6 Rotate your text, using the green circular handle on the WordArt text. Use the mouse to drag the handle in the direction you want to rotate the text. You'll see the outline of your WordArt object move. Drop the green circle and your text will be redrawn in the new position.

7 Experiment with the other effects on the toolbar. Here, we've clicked on the WordArt Same Letter Heights button, fourth from the right (inset), which stretches lower case letters to the same height as capital letters.

8 You can change the position of the WordArt object in your document by dragging and dropping it. You'll notice that as your mouse passes over the object, it changes to a four-headed arrow to show that you can move it around in your document. Notice that because we selected a top and bottom wrap for the object, the document text reflows around it each time we move it.

9 Why don't you try another special effect? The button on the extreme right controls how close together the text characters appear. We have shown the effect of the Very Tight character spacing option in this final example.

Adding graphics with clip art

To add character to your documents, why not insert a picture? You'll find that a great selection of ready-to-use illustrations is supplied with your Word software.

1 Type in some text for another invitation. This time you can use some clip art to illustrate it. Make sure the Task Pane is visible (select Task Pane on the View menu, if necessary) and select Insert **Clip Art** from the drop-down menu at the top of the Task Pane.

2 The first time you do this, Word suggests cataloguing the Multimedia file on your hard disk. Click the Now button. Wait a few moments as Word indexes the files it finds.

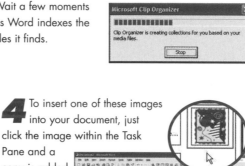

3 In the Insert Clip Art Task Pane, type a suitable search term into the Search For box. Then click the Search button. Word looks through the catalogue it has created and shows thumbnail images for all matching clip art images.

4 To insert one of these images into your document, just click the image within the Task Pane and a copy is added to your document.

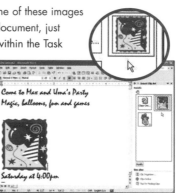

5 If the image isn't quite the right size, you can change it by moving any of the six handles that appear along the edges of the

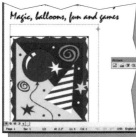

image when it is selected. Click once and these small black squares appear; drag one of these handles. A dotted outline shows the image's new size – just release the mouse button when it's the right size.

6 While an image is selected, the floating Picture toolbar lets you adjust its appearance. For example, you can create a watermark-style image by selecting Washout from the menu that appears when you click on the second button on the toolbar. Experiment with the other options – if you make a mistake, the button at the far right of the toolbar resets the image to its original state.

7 You can also browse for images using the Clip Organizer window. First, click on Clip Organizer near the bottom of the Insert Clip Art Task Pane.

8 The Clip Organizer window lets you look through all the images on your computer. If your copy of Word is part of the Microsoft Office suite of programs, you can look through the many categories in the Office Collections folder, for example. To add an image to your document, simply click any of the thumbnail images that appear on the panel on the right.

Inserting your own graphics to create a unique letterhead

For the ultimate in personalization, you can use pictures created in programs such as Paint to illustrate and decorate your Word letters.

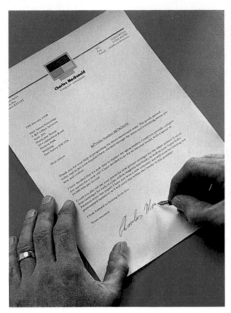

Letterheads really benefit from the custom-made look. Create your own distinctive logo and insert it into your letters.

YOU'VE SEEN how you can add text effects and clip art graphics to your Word documents. But there will always be occasions when you can't quite find the right piece of clip art for a particular document. If this is the case, the only thing to do is create the image in a graphics program and insert it into your Word letter. This way you can create exactly the picture you want and make your documents stand out from those made with standard clip art.

We'll show you how to create your own pictures using Paint on pages 64–65. In the meantime you can use any bitmap in the following step-by-step guide.

● Adding a logo

One example of how to use your own drawings is to create your own letterhead to make your letters more attractive and individual. Try different types of logo before choosing one.

As with WordArt and clip art graphics, Word gives you plenty of control over how your own pictures appear in documents. In fact, you can do everything to your drawing that you can do to a piece of clip art. You can position your drawings precisely, change their shape and size and specify how text should wrap round them.

Adding a logo from Paint to a Word document

If you can insert clip art into your Word documents, you'll find that it's just as easy to add pictures you've created yourself to a document. Here we make an attractive, customized letterhead.

1 To start off our letterhead, we've typed some typical name, address and contact details at the top of our page. Then we've clicked on the Insert menu, the Picture command and then the From File option.

2 An Insert Picture dialog box appears. To insert a logo created in Paint, click on the Look in: box and select the (C:) drive. Select a folder containing a Paint file – we are using the 'paint-logo.bmp' file. The files in the folder appear as a set of thumbnail images. Select one and click the Insert button. (See pages 64–65 for details of how to create a logo in Paint.)

3 The image will be pulled into your document and a floating Picture toolbar appears if you click on the image. Don't worry if your text has wrapped oddly around the logo: click the Text Wrapping button and choose the Through option from the drop-down list of commands that appear.

4 Use the handles on the logo's edges to make it smaller, then drag it to the top of the page. Depending on your logo and the information in your letterhead, other layouts may work better. Once you are happy with your letterhead, save it as a template (see pages 38–41). That way you can use it whenever you write a letter.

Spreadsheets made easy

Confused by the very idea of a spreadsheet? Not even sure what a spreadsheet is? Here's a straightforward introduction to one of the most useful PC programs.

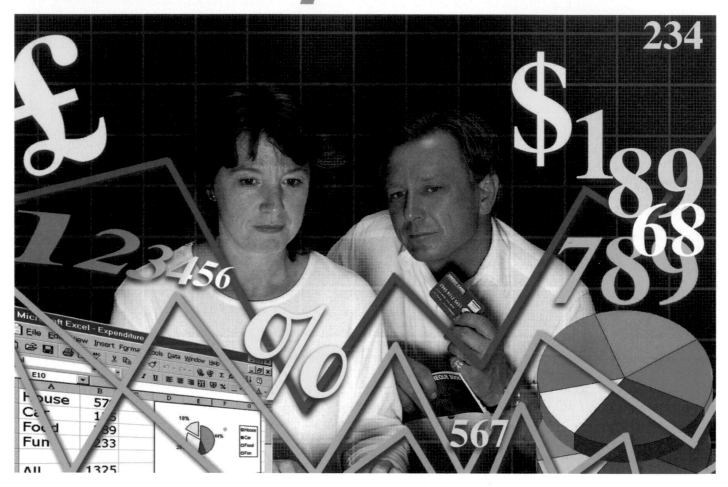

If you thought spreadsheets were only for accountants and other number crunchers, think again. Today's spreadsheets are so flexible even home PC users can use them to tackle any number of domestic chores, such as tracking your bank balance, working out expense claims and even helping with school work.

You can do so much with a spreadsheet that it is hard to explain with a single example. Unlike a word processor, which is like an advanced typewriter, the spreadsheet has no simple equivalent. Instead, it is a unique and powerful combination of different tools.

To start with, a spreadsheet is stuffed full with the maths capabilities of an advanced calculator, but even better, it can also make

stunning graphs with a few mouse clicks. It is laid out in a table of rows and columns so it looks a little like an accountant's ledger book. But unlike a book, you can add new rows and columns as it suits you, without tearing the whole thing up and starting from scratch.

Best of all, if you want to see the effect that a change in one of the numbers you have entered has on the rest, you need only alter a single number and the spreadsheet will perform the calculations for you.

● Rows and columns
Rather like the grid you use when you're playing the children's game Battleships, each column of the spreadsheet has a letter heading (A, B, C, ...) and each row is

Getting to grips with a few simple spreadsheet functions could revolutionize the way you handle your home finances.

numbered (1, 2, 3, ...). You can refer to each and every cell in the table by using its column-row co-ordinates: A1, A2, B5 or G12, for example.

The trick that lets a spreadsheet work its magic is being able to use figures in one cell of the table in calculations in other cells. For example, if you want cell A1 to show the contents of cell A2 plus the contents of cell A3, you would simply type '=A2+A3' into cell A1. You can add, subtract, divide, multiply and perform many other functions in spreadsheet calculations.

Don't panic if this sounds like the dreaded schooldays algebra. We'll take you step-by-step through all the spreadsheet uses and you'll soon wonder how you ever managed without one.

The spreadsheet – your flexible friend

From totting up your shopping bills to keeping track of all your domestic finances, spreadsheets are designed to help you sail through even the most confusing numerical and financial tasks.

Here's a spreadsheet at its simplest: a shopping list with one column (A) used for the type of item and another (B) for its price. At the bottom, there's a row for the total, and Excel calculates the total figure (in B11) by adding up all the figures in cells B2 to B10.

Sometimes looking at numbers in a graphical form can really help them make sense. Here Excel shows the domestic expenditure figures entered in column B as a pie chart. It's easy to see at a glance where the biggest slice of the family budget is going.

Spreadsheets can also help give a better understanding of maths – great for school children and adults alike. A spreadsheet's ability to show instant results in a graph without resorting to old-fashioned pencil and paper plotting encourages experimentation.

For the self-employed home PC user, a spreadsheet can be vital. Here you can see monthly income and expenses. What happens if the price of paper goes up? Just type in the new price, and you will instantly see the effect on profitability. These 'what-if?' calculations are a spreadsheet's strongest feature.

You don't have to use any calculations in your spreadsheet. Some people find that its ready-made table layout (above) makes it ideal for keeping simple lists. Here we've shown a list of contacts, one per row, with columns for names, addresses, telephone numbers etc.

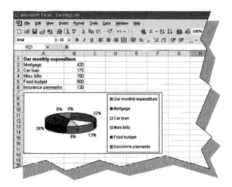

A spreadsheet doesn't always have to look like a grid. We've taken the same information from the previous example and asked Excel to show it in a form (below). Here you see one row of data at a time, and just click through the list.

The Excel worksheet

Worksheets are the documents that Excel uses to store and display information. Built from a grid of rows and columns, a worksheet is easy to understand once you know the basics. Let's get started with our step-by-step guide.

Toolbars

Excel's toolbars provide one-click access to many common commands.

Name box

The Name box displays the co-ordinates of the current cell.

Current cell

The current cell is indicated by the black highlight around it. At the same time, the relevant row and column heading are highlighted in blue.

Rows

Rows in the worksheet are identified by number.

Worksheet tab

Excel documents can contain many worksheets. You click on a tab to select each one.

Status bar

Most of the time, you'll see 'Ready' here, indicating that Excel is waiting for you to input information. Even when it's working on huge calculations, Excel rarely keeps you waiting.

Columns

Worksheet columns are referred to by letters: A to Z for the first 26 columns; then AA for the 27th, AB for the 28th and so on.

Formula bar

The Formula bar displays the contents of the current cell. If it's a formula, you see the formula rather than the answer. This lets you check your maths.

Menu bar

Like other programs, Excel has drop-down menus that list all commands. Click once on any word in the Menu bar and a list of commands drops down.

Scroll bars

To move around the worksheet, you use the scroll bars.

Task pane

Provides useful shortcuts and access to often-used commands. Its content changes according to what you are doing.

When you first start up the Excel spreadsheet, you'll notice that a grid of rectangles (or cells, as they're known) occupies most of the window. This grid is called a worksheet and an Excel document can have as many worksheets as you need.

To start Excel, click on the Windows Start button, click All Programs on the pop-up menu and Microsoft Excel from the program list. You'll see a screen like the one above.

An Excel worksheet can have up to 256 columns and 16,384 rows – that's more than enough for any home PC user! Rows are numbered from 1 to 16,384 and columns are labelled from A to Z, then AA to AZ, BA to BZ, and so on. A cell can contain almost any kind of information: text, numbers or a formula.

Entering information is easy: click on a cell and type in whatever you want. As you type, you'll see the line of information appear in the cell and in the Formula bar. Once you've

SHORT CUTS

To move quickly back to the first cell of a worksheet, A1, press [Ctrl]+[Home]. The [Home] key is to the right and a little higher than the [Enter] key.

finished typing in that cell, press the [Tab] key to move to the cell to the right or press [Enter] to move to the row below. If you notice a mistake after you've moved to a new cell, you can click on the cell and type in all the information again. A more useful way to correct mistakes, or type in a longer string of characters, is by using the Formula bar: click on a cell and the Formula bar shows its contents, click on the information in the Formula bar and you can correct the part that's wrong. Press [Enter] when you've finished. This is often much quicker than having to retype the whole cell.

Adding up with Excel

Let's start with a simple example – your supermarket bill. You can type in all the items and their prices and get Excel to add up the total for you.

WHAT IT MEANS

FORMULA

To many PC users, the word 'formula' is the one thing that makes spreadsheets seem complicated. In fact, it's really just another way of saying 'calculation'.

Here's our tip for success: when you are typing a formula into a cell, it's just like using a calculator, but instead of pressing the equals sign (=) at the end of the calculation, you begin with it.
Calculator:

number + number =
Worksheet formula:

= cell + cell

1 We're going to type the names of the items from a supermarket bill into column B and the price of each item into column C. Click on cell B2 to select it and type in the word 'Item'. Now select cell C2 and type the word 'Price'. Notice how the cell has a thick black border around it to remind you that it is the one you're working in.

2 Click on cell B3 (located directly below 'Item') to select it and type in the word 'Apples'. Now press the [Tab] key to move across to cell C3 (the one located directly below the 'Price' heading). This time type in '1.25' for the price of the apples. Don't bother with the £ sign for now – we'll cover currency fully later in the course.

3 Now keep adding more items and prices in the cells below until you've completed your list. We've included bread at 59p, wine at £4.49, cheese at £2.21 and a bar of chocolate at 35p – your list can be different.

Note: when typing amounts that are less than one pound, just type them as a decimal. For example, type '.35' for 35p.

4 Click the cell that's located below the final price you typed into your list (this is cell C8 in our example). Now insert the **formula** that adds up this list by typing: '=C3+C4+C5+C6+C7'

Each cell in the formula is given a different colour. Press the [Enter] key and Excel knows you've finished and adds up the figures. It will show the answer in place of the formula.

5 The power of spreadsheets is in their ability to do the sum again if something changes. Imagine that you mistyped the price of the wine: it was really £5.29. On a calculator you'd have to start again. In Excel, all you have to do is change the price and it will recalculate the total in a fraction of a second. Try it. Now imagine how useful this is for long lists!

Using Excel formulae

You're not just limited to simple sums with a spreadsheet – if you include other mathematical operations in your formulae, you can make Excel work harder for you and your family. Here's how to forecast your monthly food budget.

If you tried the Excel exercise on page 53, you will already have seen how Excel can save you having to do basic arithmetic. Excel has a whole range of formulae and functions so that it can carry out many more operations for all sorts of home computing tasks.

In the previous exercise, when you added up the right-hand column, you typed in '=C3+C4+C5+C6+C7', which will have been displayed in the Formula bar. All formulae look like this. They always begin with an equals sign (=) to show Excel that it is expected to perform a calculation. Then they contain the cell locations and details of the mathematical operations that you want Excel to carry out. In this case, Excel understands the calculation displayed in the Formula bar as 'add the contents of cells C3, C4, C5, C6 and C7; put the answer in the current cell'.

● Summing it up

Excel calculations can be as simple or as complicated as you want, depending on the instructions that you put in. But most of the time, they will just use the four basic arithmetic instructions that appear on a calculator: plus, minus, multiply and divide.

Unlike a calculator, however, once you have entered a formula it will stay in place in the worksheet, and if you change your data, Excel will automatically redo the calculations and tell you the new answer.

● The Formula bar

Any formula that applies to the current cell is displayed in the Formula bar (see page 52). All formulae must begin with an equals sign (=). That's how Excel knows that what follows is a formula (as opposed to a text title, such as 'Items' or 'Price', a number, such as '12' or '8.56378', or a date, such as '18/07/02').

You type the plus sign with the plus [+] key on the main keyboard or the numeric keypad. For minus, you use the hyphen [-] key or the minus [-] key on the numeric keypad.

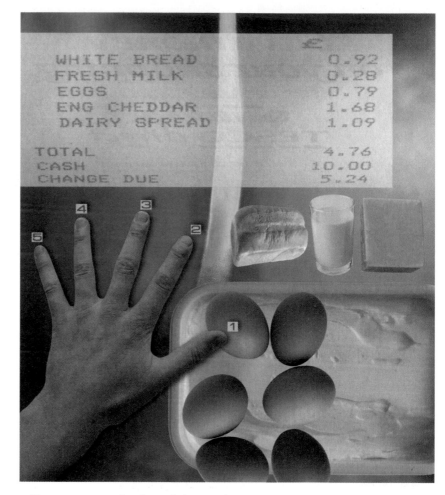

Your computer keyboard doesn't have true divide or multiply keys, so you use the forward slash key [/] for division and the asterisk [*] key for multiplication.

For example, to divide cell B2 by cell B7, you would type '=B2/B7'. To multiply cell A6 by B6, you would type '=A6*B6'. You can also use the operations in combination, too. For example, '=A2*B2/B3' would multiply A2 by B2 and divide the result by B3.

You can also use these maths operations with numbers. For example, to multiply 23 by 35, type '=23*35' straight into an Excel cell. When you press the [Enter] key, you'll get the answer. You can also combine numbers and cell locations; a formula of '=A2*1.25' multiplies the contents of cell A2 by 1.25.

Figure out your shopping bills efficiently with your own made-to-measure worksheet.

If your spreadsheet is very large, it can be quicker to move around it by using the [Page Up] and [Page Down] keys instead of clicking on the scroll bars with the mouse.

Work out your shopping budget

Calculate your month's food expenditure with Excel.

PC TIPS

There are many other useful maths operations you can get Excel to do for you. For example, if you wanted to find the square of 213, just type '=213^2' into any cell. (You type the ^ symbol by typing [Shift]+[6].)

When Excel calculates a formula, it applies the same rules that apply in normal maths, so use brackets to show which parts of a calculation should be done first, for instance.

Consider this example: '=(B2-B3)*B4'. The brackets indicate that B3 must be subtracted from B2 first, and then the result should be multiplied by B4.

Compare this to: '=B2-B3*B4'. Here, you would multiply B3 by B4 and then subtract the result from B2. The answer would be very different. Be careful not to miss out necessary brackets.

1 Start a new worksheet. We'll use column B to enter the food items and column C for their prices. Click on cell B2 to select it and type in the word 'Item'. Click on cell C2 and type in 'Prices'.

2 Now use column B to enter a range of food items, and column C for the price of each item. Don't bother with the £ or p signs; just type in 75p as '.75', and £1.73 as '1.73'.

3 Click on cell D2 and type in 'Number'. In cell D3 type in the number of loaves you buy each month – we've entered '8'. Carry on down the column, adding numbers for each item in your list.

4 Now you can use formulae to enter the calculations you want to perform. Click on cell E2 and type in 'Total'. Then click on cell E3. Type in '=C3*D3' (using the asterisk [*] key). This will multiply the number in C3 by the number in D3.

5 To see how the formula automatically recalculates for you, click on cell C3 and type in a new price: the total in cell E3 will adjust itself. Change the price back, and change the number of loaves in cell C3: again, the total will change.

6 Carry on down column E with these multiplications: in E4, enter the formula '=C4*D4', and so on. Remember: if you make a mistake just retype the cell formula again, or edit the formula on the Formula bar (see page 52).

7 When you reach the bottom of your list, use another formula to work out the total monthly bill. Type 'Monthly Total' into cell B8, then click on cell E8 and type in '=E3+E4+E5+E6+E7'. When you press the [Enter] key, you'll see the overall total. Just like other formulae, any change in prices or numbers will recalculate this figure automatically.

8 You can see how subtraction works by taking the total bill from a monthly shopping budget. Type 'Monthly Budget' in cell B9, click on cell E9 and type a figure for your monthly shopping budget (we have used '125' for £125).

Click on B10 and type in 'Monthly Surplus'. Now click on E10 and enter the formula '=E9–E8'.

9 You do division in a similar way. We will use another formula to work out approximately how much is left over each week from our monthly budget and get Excel to put the result in cell E11.

Click on E11 and type in '=E10/4' (this will divide the contents of cell E10 by 4 – a rough approximation of the weekly surplus).

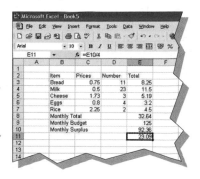

Selecting cells and moving around in Excel

To make the most of Excel worksheets, you need to know your way around Excel's most important tools. Here's a look at two of the program's most commonly used features.

At first sight, an Excel worksheet looks fairly daunting, with row upon row and column upon column of cells. However, the cells are nothing more than squares or boxes you might fill in on paper; it all looks very rigid and formal to start with, but you can type information into any box you like.

In the previous exercises, we've shown how Excel can help with simple domestic finances (see pages 53 and 55). Now, we're going to cover two vital Excel principles: how to select cells in the worksheet and how to manage your documents using the File menu.

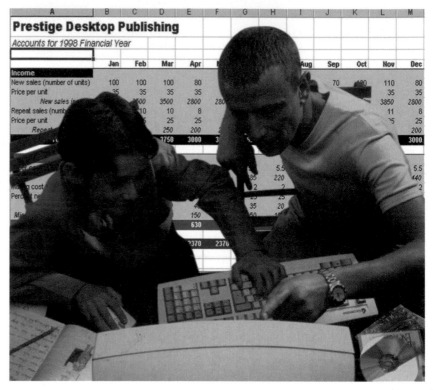

● **Selecting cells**

To select a single cell, you can simply move the mouse pointer and click on it. If you want to select a block of cells, hold down the mouse button over a cell at one corner of the block you wish to select. Then, still holding down the mouse button, drag the mouse over the other cells in the block and release the mouse button. The cells in the block will turn blue as you drag the mouse over them – this shows they are selected.

Another way to select a block of cells is to click on the cell you want to be at one corner of the block, press and hold down the [Shift] key and click again on the cell you want at the opposite corner of the selection.

● **Advanced selection**

Both of these techniques select a continuous rectangular group of cells. All the cells must be physically adjacent. Often you'll find, however, that you need to select cells that are not next to each other, perhaps if you want to select individual entries in a list. How do you select these without selecting all the others in between them?

Luckily, the programmers who made Excel thought of this. You can use the same mouse techniques together with the [Ctrl] key to

Selecting groups of cells that are not next to each other is easy – just use the [Ctrl] key and click on the cells. You'll find that any new cells you click on will be added to the existing selection.

You will find plenty of home computing jobs you can use Excel to tackle.

S H O R T C U T S

In addition to using the cursor keys to move from cell to cell, you can also use the [Enter] key. This is useful if you have just used the [Enter] key to finish typing information into a cell. The [Enter] key moves the highlight down one row. Use [Shift]+[Enter] to move up one cell.

select any cells you like. Click on the first cell you want to select. Then press and hold down the [Ctrl] key. Now click on all the other cells you want in your selection. Once the [Ctrl] key is pressed down, you can also drag the mouse to add more cells to the selection.

● Moving around a worksheet

Excel will also 'remember' your selection if you need to use the scroll bars to move around your worksheet and select yet more cells. Select your first group of cells, use the mouse on the scroll bars until you can see the new cells you want to add, and use the [Ctrl] key technique as before.

When creating a complicated selection, beware of accidentally clicking on a cell without pressing the [Ctrl] key – your whole selection will be lost!

PC TIPS

You can select every cell in the worksheet by clicking on the blank button at the top left, where the column and row headings meet. When you click on the button, the whole spreadsheet becomes highlighted. You can now carry out the same operations on the whole worksheet as you would on individual cells, such as changing the typeface.

A look down Excel's File menu

In Excel's File menu you will find the commands that allow you to open and save worksheets, and many other useful tools too; the most common ones have shortcut keystroke commands shown alongside.

The New command will create a new blank worksheet. You can work on several worksheets at a time.

Use the Open command to re-open a worksheet you have already created and worked on.

The Close command closes the current worksheet. If you have made changes, but have not yet saved your work, Excel will prompt you to save before closing the file.

The first three commands are used when preparing to print your worksheets. We shall cover them in depth later. The Print command sends a copy of the current worksheet to the printer.

The Send To command is primarily aimed at business users who can send worksheets to each other over their office networks.

Excel lists the last few files on which you have been working. You can open them by clicking on the entry here instead of using the Open command – it's much quicker.

The last command is in a group of its own: clicking on Exit closes Excel. You will be prompted to save your work if any of the open worksheets have changed since the last save.

Use Save to save your work. It will save your changes to the current file, keeping the same file name and location. If your file does not yet have a name, Excel will prompt you to choose one. The Save As command differs from Save because it lets you save the file with a different name and/or save it to a different disk location (perhaps to a floppy disk for taking into the office).

The Save as Web Page and Web Page Preview commands let you turn your spreadsheet into a Web page and check its appearance.

Save Workspace allows you to save a whole group of files and the way they appear on screen. This is useful if you regularly work with the same set of files – a complete home budget, for example.

If you select the Search command, Excel brings up a Task Pane that lets you search your hard disk for documents containing specific phrases.

The Properties command will tell you about the current worksheet, for example, what day and time the file was created and how many worksheets it contains.

Styling and colouring your spreadsheets

We've already seen ways to liven up text in Word letters and documents, but you can do the same to your spreadsheets to make them more attractive and easier to read. Here's how to add colour and pizzazz to your Excel worksheets.

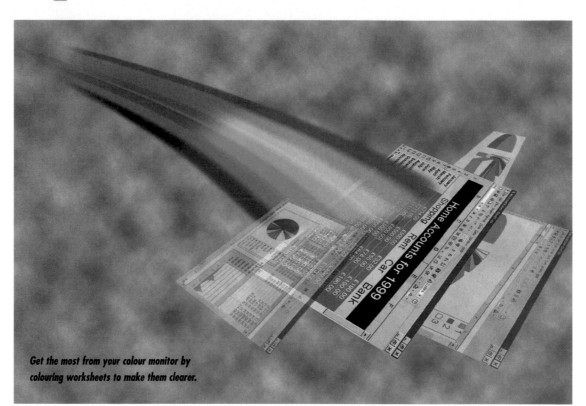

Get the most from your colour monitor by colouring worksheets to make them clearer.

In the Word exercises, we've seen how to add spice to a letter (see pages 36–37). This makes it more pleasing to the eye and helps get the right message across. The same principles apply to Excel – indeed, many would argue that the standard white cells crammed with black figures are in desperate need of livening up!

Excel tries to guess how you want the information in your worksheet laid out: it aligns words to the left, and numbers to the right. If you want something more fancy, then you must do it yourself. Don't be put off – it's easy to do, and worth the effort.

The second of Excel's toolbars provides point-and-click access to most of the popular cell formatting commands. Some tools are similar to those of Word; others are specific to Excel. Pause with the mouse over each tool to get a quick description of what it does.

As we've seen in Word, formatting text is easy. You can change the alignment, size, typeface and weight of words and numbers. Many of Excel's tools are exactly the same as those in Word (see below). You can also change the height of rows and width of columns to squeeze in more information.

● A touch of colour

It's also simple to add colour to your worksheet – just highlight the cells you want to change and click on the Fill Color and Font Color tools (the two buttons at the far right of the toolbar).

Changing the filled colour of worksheet cells can be used to great effect. Even if you don't have a colour printer, just using colour on screen can make spreadsheets easier to work with.

Arial ▾ 10 ▾ **B** *I* U ▦ ▤ ▤ ▦ ⬚ % , +.0 .00 ⠿ ⠿ ⬚ ▾ ▨ ▾ A ▾

Underline

Adding clarity

Make your worksheets easier to understand and help to get your point across by styling and formatting the text, adding colour and resizing cells.

SHORT CUTS

Excel responds to many of the same shortcuts that other Windows programs do. For instance, to get bold text, you don't need to move your mouse up to the toolbar. First, select the cells in which you want the text to be bold, then press [Ctrl]+[B].

You can also change text to italics by pressing [Ctrl]+[I] and underline text by pressing [Ctrl]+[U]. To reverse any of these actions, just press the same keys again.

1 Here's how a simple record of quarterly bills might look typed straight into Excel. All the information is there, but it's not easy to follow, so let's do something to make it clearer.

2 We want to make sure that the headings for the bills and the quarters of the year are prominent. Select the cells and press the Bold button.

3 Now we can see that some of the text in some of the cells in the B column is obscured by the C column. To increase the width of column B, move the

mouse to the border between the B and the C column buttons. Notice that it changes to a double-headed arrow. Click and drag to the right to make the column wider; you'll see a vertical dotted line indicating the new width of the column.

4 Add cell borders to divide the different parts of the table: select the top row of cells and click on the down arrow by the Borders button. Select the thick black bottom border from the choice of borders. Do the same for the sixth row, with the thinner border.

5 Select the headings again and click on the down arrow next to the Font Color tool. A palette of different coloured squares pops up (right). Click over the white one. As you do, you'll notice that your text seems to disappear. It's still there, but you can't see white text on a white background.

6 Now click the down arrow next to the Fill Color tool. Another colour palette pops up: click on the bright red one. Notice that your white text is now visible against the darker background.

7 Now colour the cells for the other rows in the same way. We've chosen matching colours for the other rows to minimize eyestrain. (Note: when working on very wide tables of information, it's helpful to choose alternating colours for the rows to help you read across the table.)

8 Now select all the number cells. We want to show that these figures represent money by using Excel's Currency tool. It's in the centre of the toolbar and its icon shows banknotes and coins (left). Click on the button and Excel gets the right currency symbol by checking your Windows country settings (we'll discuss these later in the course). It then uses the symbol and adds two decimal places for smaller denominations.

9 Now that we've increased the amount of information in the cells, the cells are looking a little crowded. First we need to select all four columns, C to F, at the same time. To do this move the mouse over the column C button, click and hold the button down and then drag the pointer across the other three columns. You'll see the columns become highlighted.

10 Let go of the mouse (the four columns stay highlighted) and use the column dragging technique (step 3). As you drag, you'll see a dotted line (left) that shows how wide your columns will

be. Release the mouse and you'll see that Excel widens all four columns at once. Finally, select the quarterly period cells and use the Align Right button to make them sit over the cost figures (above).

Presenting pie charts

A colourful three-dimensional pie chart is a great way to clearly display the information contained in lists of figures. It can be easy and fun to present your household finances in this pictorial form, so even children will be able to appreciate how the family budget works.

There are few things more daunting than trying to understand what is really happening in a complicated set of figures. Scientists, engineers and business people frequently convert numbers into charts and graphs to make it easier to see at a glance what's going on.

You can borrow this professional technique when you want to analyze the information you store in your spreadsheets at home. What's more, a spreadsheet makes it easy to produce impressive and expert-looking results straightaway. But the best aspect of using a spreadsheet is that the labour-intensive chore of drawing the graph is taken out of your hands and performed quickly and accurately by your computer.

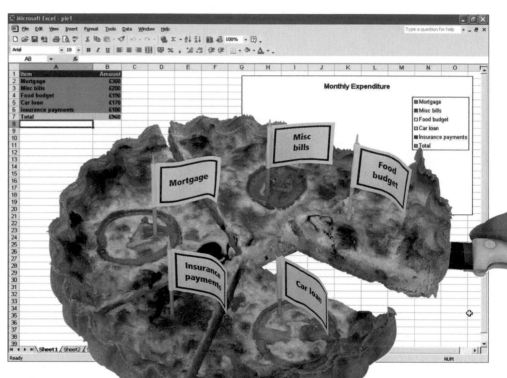

Pie charts display the family finances clearly enough for everyone to appreciate.

● A wizard with numbers

Excel has a tool called the Chart Wizard that will lead you through a step-by-step process to create a chart or graph from any figures in your spreadsheet. In only a few steps, you can make colourful pie charts, bar graphs or line graphs. For a more artistic touch, you can choose 3D pie charts, cylinders and pyramids.

For any of these charts, you can choose the colours of each part, make notes and add headings. Once you've created your chart, you can position it anywhere you like in a document, resize it or put it on a page of its own. If you decide you don't like the way your chart looks, you can change it by using the Chart toolbar or the Chart menu.

● Automatic updates

Perhaps the most powerful feature of charting in Excel is that you don't have to make a new chart every time you change a figure – your chart is dynamically linked to

For the professional touch, Excel can show the 'slices' of a pie chart in three dimensions and a range of different colours.

the cells that hold the figures used to create it. In other words, every time you modify one of the cells used in your chart, Excel will automatically redraw the chart to show the effects. Experiment with this function when you've worked through the example opposite. The maroon coloured slice of the 3D pie chart in the example represents the £300 mortgage payment. Imagine that there's a change in interest rates and your mortgage repayment goes down to £250.

Click on the cell containing the mortgage figure and type in '250'. Watch to see what happens to the pie chart when you press the [Enter] key. The pie chart is redrawn almost instantly to reflect the change you've just made to the figures.

How to create your first pie chart

In this step-by-step example, you'll find out how to use Excel to create a colourful three-dimensional pie chart to show how a typical household budget is sliced up.

PC TIPS

Zoom factor

To change the amount of the worksheet you can see, alter the zoom factor. Look along Excel's top toolbar and towards the right hand end you'll see the Zoom button with a 100% figure next to it. Click once to see the drop-down menu of options, or click on the 100% figure in the toolbar to type another number. If you can't see the Zoom button on the toolbar, click the Toolbar Options button at the far right of the toolbar.

1 Type in some figures to represent the major areas of domestic expenditure, with labels and headings as shown here. We've formatted our table of figures with two colours to make them stand out from the white worksheet (see pages 58–59).

2 Now tell Excel what information you want to include in your pie chart. Select the table by dragging the mouse from the top left cell to the bottom right cell – the cells will be highlighted. Remember to include the two column headings as well as all the descriptions and amounts, as these will also appear on your pie chart.

3 To chart your information, we'll use Excel's Chart Wizard tool. You start it by clicking on the small graph button towards the right of the toolbar.

4 The first step in the Chart Wizard lets you choose the exact type of chart you want to create. If you click on items in the Chart type list in the column on the left side of the dialog box, the Chart sub-types on the right shows previews of the options available with these types of chart.

Click on Pie in the Chart type list, then click on the picture in the middle of the top row (showing a three-dimensional pie chart) of the Chart sub-types. Then click on Next.

5 On the next screen, tell the Chart Wizard which data you want to use. We've already highlighted the relevant cells (see step 2) so just click Next. Name your chart 'Monthly Expenditure' in the Chart title text box and click OK.

6 Next, the Chart Wizard asks you to choose between showing your pie chart as a completely new worksheet or as a 'floating' object on the page where the table of figures is. Make sure that the As object in: option is selected and click on the Finish button.

7 Excel immediately draws the pie chart on your worksheet. You can make the pie chart larger or smaller by moving the small black handles on the edges of the chart. You can move the whole chart by dragging and dropping it with the mouse pointer.

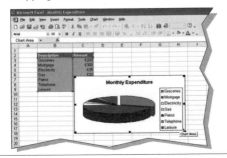

8 When you click on the pie chart, a Chart toolbar appears. You can modify many aspects of the chart using this, including the colours, the text and the position of any part of it. Click on the drop-down box at the left of the toolbar (below) and select Series "Amount". Now you can pull out a slice of the pie. Click on one of the pie segments to select it; you'll see some small handles appear on its edges. Use the mouse to drag it away from the rest of the pie chart.

You can also change the colour of each pie slice by using the Fill Color tool on the Formatting toolbar above the worksheet area (see pages 58–59).

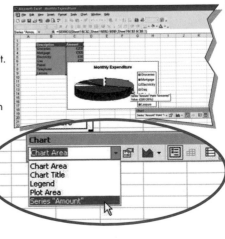

Adding with AutoSum

We've already seen how easy it is to use Excel to add up a few numbers quickly. Now let's find out the most efficient and accurate way of dealing with much larger sets of figures.

You already know how to use a simple formula to add up a small set of figures, such as a short shopping bill (see pages 52–53). For example, if we wanted to add up the four figures in the first four cells in column C of an Excel spreadsheet, we would use the formula '=C1+C2+C3+C4'. If you put this formula into cell C5, that's where Excel would put the result.

This manual method of typing in the whole formula, including all the cells you want, is fine when you only want to add up a short set of figures, but what happens when you want to add up the contents of 30 or 40 cells? It would be tiresome to type in all the cell names to make up the formula – and you would probably make mistakes along the way. Luckily, Excel includes a tool called AutoSum that takes the hassle out of this chore.

● **Quick and easy**
Here's a simple example of how AutoSum works: let's imagine that you have a column of 20 numbers in cells C1 through to C20 and

you want to add them up and put the result in cell C21. First, click over cell C21 to select it and then move up to the Standard toolbar (usually the row of tools directly underneath the menu options). Locate the AutoSum tool (it looks like the capital Greek letter sigma Σ) and click on it. A flashing dotted line will appear around cells C1 through to C20 and a formula like this will appear in cell C21: '=SUM(C1:C20)'. Simply press the [Enter] key to finish the job and the result will appear in cell C21.

● **Mind the gaps**
As you can see, it's quick and easy to do, but you should still take a little care because sometimes Excel has to make guesses about which cells you want to include in your sum.

Let's imagine that there wasn't a number in cell C9 in the previous example. Then Excel would guess that you only wanted to add up the contents of cells C10 through to C20 because of the gap made by the empty C9 cell. Instead of pressing the [Enter] key immediately, you would have to drag and drop with the mouse to select all the cells

between C1 and C20 and then press [Enter].

Excel would make the same sort of guess if cell C9 contained any non-numerical data. So if there was text, or even another formula in cell C9, Excel would assume that this cell was the top end of the column of figures you wanted to add up and would only include cells C10 to C20 in its automatic formula.

The AutoSum tool, situated in Excel's top toolbar and represented by the Greek letter sigma, is a useful feature when you need to add up a long column of numbers.

It's always a good idea to check the total of the entries on your credit card statement – a task that can be achieved easily and accurately by using Excel.

Checking your credit card bill

See how AutoSum can make adding up a list of numbers so easy. Let's use a ready-made long number list with which many people are familiar – the credit card bill.

WHAT IT MEANS

FUNCTION

Excel uses special commands called functions to work out results from data that appears in brackets after the function. For example, 'SUM(1,2,3)' adds up 1, 2 and 3 to get 6. Excel understands a huge range of functions, including those that work out mathematical problems and calculate statistics.

1 Here's a typical set of monthly credit card expenses. Open a worksheet and copy the information shown here exactly. We could create a long formula by hand in cell D22 to add them up, but the problem is that there are 18 number entries here and it would be tedious to type in the whole formula.

2 Let's use Excel's AutoSum feature instead. Click over cell D22 and then click over the AutoSum tool (this is the letter ∑ in the top toolbar). Excel only selects the cells from D13 onwards because it thinks the text in D12 is the top end of the column of figures you want to add up.

3 Press the [Esc] key to cancel the AutoSum. Now change the word 'Fifty' to the number '50' and try again. Click on cell D22 and click the AutoSum tool. This time Excel thinks you want to add up the contents of cells D10 to D21 because cell D9 is empty. It sees an empty cell as the end of a column of figures.

4 You can use the drag and drop technique with your mouse to change the cells automatically selected by Excel. With the dotted outline still showing, click over cell D4, hold down the left mouse button and drag down to select all of the cells from D4 to D21. Release the mouse button when you've finished.

5 Now press the [Enter] key to tell Excel that you've finished selecting the cells. The spreadsheet automatically adds up the column of figures in the cells D4 to D21 and places the result, '828.77', in cell D22. This way is a lot easier than typing in a formula that includes each individual cell.

6 Excel has automatically created the formula in cell D22 for you. Click over this cell and look closely at what comes up in the Formula bar: it says '=SUM(D4:D21)'. Excel has used a special **function** called SUM to save the effort of including every cell between D4 and D21 in its formula.

7 Now let's go back and fill in the missing amount for the petrol. Click on cell D9 and type in '9.50'. Now press the [Enter] key and watch what happens to the total in cell D22. Excel recalculates the sum. Now you know that the calculation by the credit card company is correct.

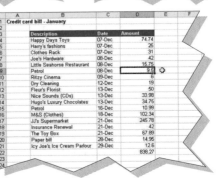

	A	B	C	D	E	F
1	Credit card bill - January					
2						
3		**Description**	**Date**	**Amount**		
4		Happy Days Toys	07-Dec	74.74		
5		Harry's fashions	07-Dec	25		
6		Clothes Rack	07-Dec	31		
7		Joe's Hardware	08-Dec	42		
8		Little Seahorse Restaurant	08-Dec	15.75		
9		Petrol	08-Dec	9.5		
10		Ritzy Cinema	09-Dec	6		
11		Dry Cleaning	12-Dec	19		
12		Fleur's Florist	13-Dec	6		
13		Nice Sounds (CDs)	13-Dec	33.98		
14		Hugo's Luxury Chocolates	13-Dec	34.75		
15		Petrol	16-Dec	10.99		
16		M&S (Clothes)	18-Dec	102.34		
17		JJ's Supermarket	21-Dec	245.78		
18		Insurance Renewal	21-Dec	42		
19		The Toy Box	21-Dec	67.89		
20		Paper bill	26-Dec	14.95		
21		Icy Joe's Ice Cream Parlour	29-Dec	12.6		
22				838.27		
23						
24						

First steps in graphics

The Microsoft Paint program is supplied with Windows. In the following series of tutorials, you'll find out how easy it is to create your own pictures.

Making graphics (or pictures) is one of the most creatively rewarding activities you can do with your computer. You don't even need to buy an expensive graphics program because Windows already includes an ideal one for beginners, Microsoft Paint.

Apart from being free with Windows, Paint has the great advantage of simplicity. It's the ideal way to get to grips with the basic graphics tools without being bewildered by the vast array of features offered by the more advanced graphics programs.

Start Paint by clicking on the Start button, then All Programs, then Accessories and then clicking on the Paint option.

A tour around the Paint window

Toolbox
Paint has plenty of tools to use in your pictures. On the opposite page, you get to use the shape drawing and paint filling tools.

The lower part of the toolbox changes to give you more options, depending on the tool you chose.

Palette
Just as real painters work with a palette of colours, so does Microsoft Paint.

Menu bar
Paint has six menu items. Click on a word to see the list of commands under each subject heading.

Scroll bars
You can move around a big picture by moving the scroll bars.

Status bar
The bar at the very bottom of the window shows extra information about a picture.

Creating a coloured logo

Imagine that a computer salesman friend has asked you to design a new logo for his business. His idea is a computer monitor split into four colourful rectangles. Here's how to paint it on your PC.

❶ Click the toolbox button with the rectangle outline to select the Rectangle drawing tool.

❷ Click on the middle rectangle below the toolbox to choose a filled box with a border.

❸ Select the border colour: click on black in the palette with the LEFT mouse button.

❹ Fill the rectangle with colour: click on grey in the palette with the RIGHT mouse button.

❺ You will now see a black rectangle on top of a grey one just to the left of the palette.

❻ Now go to the white drawing area. Click, and keeping the left mouse button pressed, drag the pointer across and down the screen until you're happy with the shape and let go.

❼ Use the mouse to draw another, smaller rectangle underneath the large one, as in step 6. This will represent the monitor stand.

❽ Click on the Rounded Rectangle button at the bottom of the toolbox.

❾ To fill the rectangle with the colour white, click on the white box in the palette with the RIGHT mouse button.

❿ Move to the drawing area and draw the screen just inside the grey area, which represents the surround of the monitor.

⓫ Select the Line tool.

⓬ Move the pointer to the top of the screen, and draw by holding down the left mouse button as you move the mouse downwards.

Press and hold the [Shift] key while drawing the line to keep it perfectly straight.

⓭ Draw a horizontal line across the screen of your monitor picture in the same way.

⓲ Now save the picture. Click on the File menu and click on Save.

⓮ Click on the purple square in the palette to change the paint colour.

⓯ Return to the toolbox and click on the tipping paint pot. This Fill With Color tool fills an area of one colour with another colour.

⓰ Move to the drawing area and click in the white top left quarter of the screen. This will fill this quarter of the screen with the purple paint you chose in step 14.

⓱ Now apply other colours to the other three quarters of the monitor screen. You can use the Fill With Color tool as often as you like – just choose the colour from the palette.

If you find paint 'leaks' from one quarter of the screen into another, check for small gaps at either end of the lines you have drawn. Paint can flow through the tiniest holes. If you find one, use the Line tool to extend it.

⓳ Type a name for the picture.

⓴ Click on the Save button. The default folder for Paint images is My Pictures. See page 49 to add a Paint logo to a letterhead in Word.

Writing with Paint

Graphics programs are perfect for pictures, but some of the best results come when combining pictures and words. Here's how to use Paint's text tricks to enhance your logos and graphics.

W e've already seen that Paint provides a wide range of painting tools. An added bonus is that it also gives you the basic tools you need to add words to your pictures. Here we'll show you how to position words exactly where you want them, choose the colour and size of the letters and decide the typeface the words appear in.

There are two important tools for controlling the way your text appears: the Text tool and Text toolbar (shown opposite). Select the Text tool by clicking on the toolbar button marked with a capital A. Move into the painting area and see the pointer change shape and become a cross. Click on the position you want your text to appear in. A rectangular text box appears, containing a flashing text cursor. Type some text into this box. The box gets deeper as you type more text, but not wider. You can widen it by dragging with the mouse. Press and hold the left mouse button on the text box's corner or side squares and move the mouse down and to the right to create a bigger text box.

When creating text in Paint you need to make sure that there are no mistakes and that you are happy with the type size and shape of your text box. This is because as soon as you click outside the text box area or change from the Text tool, you cannot go back and change it with the Text tool.

● **Colourful language**
You can choose the colour of the text and its background. Use the left mouse button to click on a colour for text in the colour palette and the right mouse button to choose the colour for the box. If you don't want a solid background, for example, if you want to put words on top of a picture, make the box's background transparent. Click on the lower of the two buttons in the lower section of the Paint toolbar after you click the Text tool.

Simple doodles, sketches on your computer or formal designs of print quality are easily achievable using a graphics program, such as Microsoft Paint.

PC TIPS

multicolour!

Once you have added words to your painting, you can use other Paint tools on them. For example, you can use the Fill With Color tool to colour in individual letters after you've placed them in your painting. If you plan to do this, use a chunky font (like Impact, above) to make sure that you can select them with the Fill With Color tool. Slim letters are difficult to select and you may find yourself colouring the background instead.

Be wary of paint that leaks from letters into the rest of your picture: the fill affects all adjacent areas of the same colour. If the worst happens, and paint does leak out of the letters, you can click on Edit in the Menu bar and then select Undo to remove the effects of your Fill With Color command.

SHORT CUTS

There may be times when you want to paint using the maximum possible area of the screen. Press [Ctrl]+[L] to remove the colour palette and [Ctrl]+[T] to hide the toolbar. You now have almost the whole screen area for painting. Whenever you want to see the palette and toolbar again, just press the same keyboard shortcuts to bring them back into view.

Adding text to a painting

In the exercise on page 65, we created a colourful logo for a computer salesman. Here's how to use Paint's built-in text capabilities to add name and contact details to the painting to simulate a business card layout.

① **②**

We'll start by opening the computer screen logo we created in the last exercise (see page 65).
① Click on the word File on the Menu bar.
② Click on Open.

④ **⑤** **③**

The Open dialog box is very similar to the Save dialog box.
③ Scroll bars appear if you have many items in your folder.
④ Click on 'paint-logo'.
⑤ Click on the Open button. After a moment, your logo appears in the Paint window.

⑥

⑥ Maximize the Paint window to fill the screen. You can then see and use the area to the side of the logo.

⑧ **⑦** **⑩** **⑨**

⑦ Choose a colour for your text from the palette.
⑧ Click on the Text tool (shown by the letter A).
⑨ This panel shows the **pixel** co-ordinates of your pointer change as you move it around the painting area.
⑩ Click and drag an area for the first text line, making a note of the first number (the X co-ordinate) in the panel.

PIXEL
Your painting is composed of thousands of dots, one next to the other. These dots are called picture elements, or 'pixels'.

A painting that is 640 dots wide and 480 tall has 307,200 pixels. Paint, like most graphics programs, works with pixel co-ordinates to indicate position. For example, the third pixel in from the left on the fourth line of pixels has the co-ordinates 3,4.

Often, when drawing lines, adding text or moving parts of the picture around, you need to position items precisely, so you'll want to make a note of the co-ordinates each time.

If you can't see the Fonts toolbar (shown above), you need to use Paint's menus to make it appear.
⑪ Click on the word View in the Menu bar.
⑫ Click Text Toolbar from the drop-down list.

⑪ **⑫**

⑬ Type a name.
⑭ Click on the typeface list and choose a prominent font.
⑮ Click on the size list to change the size.

⑭ **⑬** **⑮**

Charles MacDonald

⑲ **⑱** **⑳** **⑯** **⑰**

⑯ Draw another text box.
⑰ Keep an eye on the first number in the co-ordinates panel to make sure it's exactly the same as in step 10.
⑱ Type the job title.
⑲ Choose a colour from the colour palette.
⑳ Use the Italics button to change the job title text.

㉑ Add text for the other information – address, telephone number, etc. – in the same way, making sure to use the same X co-ordinate each time.

If you make a mistake, don't worry – you can always paint a white rectangle to cover up any errors, and try again (see page 65 for details of how to use the Rectangle drawing tool).

Charles MacDonald
Computer consultant
53 Southview Drive
Eastcliff-On-Sea
West sussex
EA9 6YT

TEL: 01234 987564
FAX: 01234 987655
email: chas@macdee.com

㉑

Drawing freehand

Paint's freehand drawing power and its wide range of colour effects can be used to create simple pictures very quickly. This project shows how to design a football strip.

W e've already seen that with Microsoft Paint it's easy to draw shapes and fill them in with any colour. The next trick to learn is freehand drawing – using the mouse to draw the outline of your shapes instead of using ready-made circles and rectangles.

Freehand drawing on your computer is one of those skills that is easy to learn, but hard to master. At its simplest, you can start by doodling: draw some simple lines and curves and try to get the hang of moving the mouse while looking at the screen.

● **Getting started**

You can draw freehand using the Pencil tool or the Brush tool. In this exercise, we'll use the Brush (right) and start with a simple exercise to show basic drawing principles. With practice, a clean mouse (see page 93) and patience, you'll soon get the hang of it.

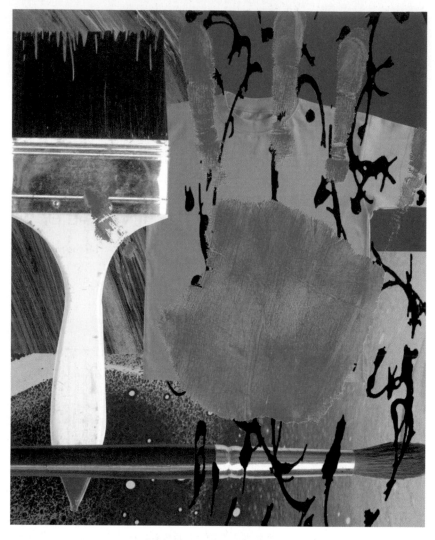

USING THE ERASER TOOL

Drawing freehand can be quite tricky at first – you'll often find that you're not as adept with your mouse as you are with a real paintbrush.

As usual, practice makes perfect, but in the meantime, you'll probably need to use the Eraser tool. This helps you correct any mistakes by rubbing out areas in your painting – you control how much or how little. In the drawing of a T-shirt (far right), the line we've drawn for the left shoulder is too long. Here's how to erase it:

1. Move the pointer onto the toolbox and click on the Eraser (right), second from the top on the left-hand side.

2. A box displaying different eraser sizes appears below the toolbox. Click on the second one down so that it is highlighted, and move your mouse over the drawing. The

pointer becomes a small square to show that the Eraser is active.

3. Position the square over the part of the image that you want to erase. Hold down the left or right mouse button and drag the mouse carefully to erase – as you would using a rubber eraser on a pencil drawing.

4. You can use the colour palette to select the colour for the erased area. For example, for a white background, you would click the right mouse button on white in the palette.

You'll find that Paint's brushes are a lot more versatile than the real thing! You can change their shape and size instantly, and there's no messy cleaning to worry about.

Drawing a football strip

Here's how to use your computer to draw and colour simple freehand shapes. We've used a football strip example to show you how to achieve fast results with the paintbrush.

Microsoft® Paint

❶ Click on the Brush icon in the toolbox. A panel appears below with brush options.

❷ Click on the middle dot in the top row of brush shapes which appear below the toolbox. This sets the width and shape of the brush.

❸ Move the mouse pointer to where you want to begin drawing the T-shirt – near the top of the screen so that you leave enough space for a pair of shorts below.

❹ Hold down the left mouse button and, using smooth and easy movements, practise drawing the scoop neck of a T-shirt.

❺ When you have completed the outline, release the mouse button. Don't worry about getting things perfect right now – you can undo your last three changes, one at a time, by pressing the [Ctrl] and [Z] keys together. Or you can use the Eraser for minor corrections.

❻ Once you are comfortable using the mouse to draw, add the sleeves and the outline of the body in the same way.

❼ If there are any gaps in your drawing, it's a simple matter to correct them; just go back and use the brush to join up the gap.

❽ Now move the pointer below the T-shirt. Hold down the left button and, in the same way you did with the T-shirt, draw the shorts.

❾ Click on a colour from the palette at the bottom of the screen. Let's try the bright red on the bottom row. (You will see red in the front square to the left of the palette to indicate that it is the active colour.)

❿ Go back to the toolbox and click on the Fill With Color tool (the tipping paint pot).

⓫ Move the paint pot cursor inside the outline of the T-shirt and press once on the left mouse button. The T-shirt fills with your chosen colour.

⓬ Repeat steps 9 to 11 for the shorts, using the dark blue from the bottom row of the palette.

⓭ Of course, you can go back to the freehand paintbrush at any time you like – even after you've filled in the T-shirt. Here we've added some vertical stripes with the paintbrush.

⓮ Then we filled alternate stripes with yellow to create a football strip look.

You can experiment with the colours of the shorts and the T-shirt as often as you wish, simply repeating steps 9 to 13 and picking up a different colour from the palette.

PC TIPS

For some drawings, the freehand outlines can make your pictures look a little chunky and childish. If you want to avoid these outlines altogether, then just draw your original outline in the paint colour you will eventually use to fill it.

If you're not sure what colour you want, but you just want to get drawing, you can use Paint's Fill With Color tool after you've drawn the line. The Fill With Color tool will fill all adjacent pixels of any colour with a new colour. So if you want to get rid of a black outline on the blue shorts, just choose the blue in the palette, click on the Fill With Color tool and click once on the black border.

Get rid of unwanted outlines by using the Fill With Color tool to fill them to match the colour that is inside the object.

Paint your own Windows Desktop

If you're bored with your standard Windows Desktop, why not create your own? With Paint, you can draw a new background pattern and cover your Desktop with it. Here's how.

Whenever your PC is switched on, Windows checks to see if you want a background design on your Desktop. Even if you haven't chosen one yourself, you might find that your PC manufacturer installed one for you.

Sometimes, new computers are set to show the Windows landscape or shaded green Windows XP background on the Desktop. Often, there is no image at all, just a solid colour. Whatever you see on your Desktop, you're not stuck with it for ever – personalizing your computer by creating your own background with Microsoft Paint is quite straightforward.

Just like real wallpaper, the overall effect is created by repeating a pattern both horizontally and vertically. Making patterns in Paint is simple and there's no reason why you can't have different background every day. It's down to your imagination.

You don't have to be a great artist to liven up your work place – even simple images look stunning when repeated all over your Desktop.

Redecorating your computer

Like the paper on your living room wall, Desktop backgrounds can really change your PC's personality. Here's how four simple Windows designs alter the look and feel of the same computer.

Contemporary Coffee Bean

Serene Greenstone

Sunny Santa Fe Stucco

Bright Blue Lace 16

Painting the Desktop

To make your own background, you first need to create your own design in Paint. After that, a simple Paint menu option will set Windows to show it on your Desktop.

1 Open the Paint program from the Windows Start menu. Before painting anything, click on the Image menu and click on the Attributes command.

2 Type in a width of 100 pixels and a height of 100 pixels to create a small square. Click the OK button.

3 Now you can start to create your basic pattern. You can use any of Paint's tools; experiment to see what works best for your type of design.

We have chosen a starfish pattern. First we filled the whole image with black paint, then we roughly painted our starfish with orange using the Airbrush tool (the fifth tool down on the left of the toolbar).

4 Now you have created your background pattern, you must save it. Select Save As from the File menu, and then save the file with a distinctive and obvious name, such as 'My Background'. Type the name you want to use in the File name: text box, and click the Save button. Now your file is saved in case you want to alter it later.

5 Paint is well integrated with Windows – it will make all the changes necessary for your pattern to appear on the Windows Desktop with just a single mouse click. All you need to do is click on the File menu and select the Set As Background (Centered) command.

6 As soon as you select this menu command, Paint will send Windows a message to add your picture to the Desktop. Click on the Paint window's Minimize button to see the effect. Your pattern appears stretched to fit the Desktop.

7 This stretched and centred picture is fine if you ever want to create a large painting to use as a single Desktop picture. What you really need for a simple small image such as this is to use it as a repeating pattern.

Paint also has this option covered. Click on the File menu, then choose the Set As Background (Tiled) option from the list of commands. Minimize the Paint window again to see the effect it has.

8 This time you'll see that your pattern starts in the top left corner and is repeated all the way across and down the screen. As you experiment, you'll see that some types of pattern work better than others.

Be careful about your colour choices – just as when you decorate at home, lively colours can prove tiring after a while. At least redecorating your Windows Desktop only takes moments.

PC TIPS

Painting in two colours

When you're painting in Microsoft Paint, there's a quick way to paint in two colours without having to move to and from the colour palette to keep switching colours. First, use the left mouse button to select one colour from the palette, then use the right mouse button to choose the other – you'll see the two colours you choose displayed on the left of the colour palette (left). Now, when you drag your mouse to paint your image, the left mouse button will paint in one colour and the right mouse button will paint in the other.

Painting in detail

Sometimes when you want to draw very accurately, a magnifying glass and special pens or brushes are useful. Here's how to work in detail on your computer with Paint's versions of these tools.

If you've ever done any close-up and detailed drawing with normal pens and pencils, you'll know how helpful it is to have a ruler and a magnifying glass handy. It's the same when you use your computer to paint, except of course that you don't use the real-life tools. Instead, almost all graphics programs provide a way to zoom in on a painting, and show guidelines to make it easy to paint accurately.

With these tools, you can zoom in until you can see the individual pixels that make up your picture. You can then change them one by one. Combine this with guidelines available on your computer, and you have very precise control over the alignment of all the elements in your painting.

● Paint's tools
Paint's versions of these tools are the Magnifier, which lets you zoom in to show pixels up to eight times larger than normal, and a grid of pixels that you can switch on and off as required. Once zoomed in, you can edit individual pixels – this means that you can change the colour of each pixel in your painting. Of course, it would be slow to paint a whole picture like this, but it's ideal for touching up small details in an image.

● Pick out the pixels
The Magnifier tool is accessible from the toolbar on the left of the Paint window. If you want to control the zoom level

Pixels are the basic building blocks of computer pictures. Often, however, you won't even notice them until you've zoomed right in.

precisely, you can select Zoom from the View menu and choose the Custom option that allows you to specify the percentage level of magnification you want.

When you have zoomed in close, you can also turn on Paint's pixel grid. This helps you get perfect alignment in your pictures. Select Zoom from the View menu, and choose the Show Grid option.

There's also a Show Thumbnail option, which displays a small picture of your whole painting to remind you what effect the changes you make will have when you see the painting back at its normal size.

● Going in close
If Paint didn't provide these tools it would be frustrating, if not impossible, to do any close-up work. What's more, being able to zoom in is useful for more than just accurate alignment. Sometimes, when you use the Fill With Color tool to paint big areas, the colour leaks out and affects other parts of your image. Zooming in allows you to find and plug the individual pixels to close the hole.

Paint is designed to allow you to work in extreme close-up for fine detail work. Use the Zoom and Magnifier tools to change your painting pixel by pixel.

WHAT IT MEANS

GRID
Most graphics programs use the concept of a grid to help you align parts of your painting. In Paint, the grid is a set of horizontal and vertical lines you can see when you choose Show Grid from the Zoom menu under View – it looks like graph paper, and the pixels you paint fill the individual squares.

Zooming in on a picture to edit fine detail

You can achieve some truly remarkable results when you zoom in to change fine detail in a picture. By repainting individual pixels on your Desktop icons, you can even give them a whole new look!

1 Open Paint and position it so that you can see one of your shortcut icons to the left (see page 15), as shown here. Press the [PrintScreen] key (it's on the top row of your keyboard towards the right). This takes a snapshot of the whole screen, and copies it into the Clipboard (see pages 16–17).

2 Click on Paint's Edit menu and select Paste from the drop-down menu that appears.

3 You'll see the snapshot of your Windows screen appear in the Paint working area. We've used this 'screen grabbing' technique to provide a ready-made image to allow us to demonstrate how to edit individual pixels.

4 Click first on View, then Zoom and then Custom. A dialog box appears: click on the 800% option and then click on the OK button.

5 The image increases in size and now you can clearly see the individual pixels that make up the small Shortcut to My Computer icon. Select the yelllow paint colour and then use the Fill With Color and Brush tools to replace all the white pixels in the original My Computer icon with yellow paint by clicking on each pixel.

6 As you work, you'll find it's hard to imagine the effect on the normal-size image. You may be unsure about the choice of yellow paint. Click the View menu, Zoom and then select Show Thumbnail from the list. A small version of your picture appears in a window on your screen.

7 Select the olive green paint above the yellow, and replace all of the light grey pixels in the Shortcut to My Computer icon.

8 Now, as you replace the grey pixels one by one, the small thumbnail window shows how your pixel editing affects the real (i.e. normal-size) image.

9 Click on the brown paint from the far right of the palette and replace all of the dark grey pixels in the icon.

10 Notice that while the picture in the painting area still looks yellow and brown, the normal size version in the thumbnail looks a bright gold colour. This is a visual effect: the human eye doesn't see the individual yellow and brown pixels; it averages out adjacent pixels and 'sees' different colours.

11 We've continued to colour in the other icons from the Desktop, using the same colour-replacing scheme detailed above. As you can see, the result is a golden set of icons – quite impressive when you consider that they were created from mainly yellow and brown paint.

For now, save this painting using the normal File and Save As menu options. Call it 'gold icons.bmp'. Later in the course, we'll show you how to replace your standard Desktop icons with these icons (or any other images you want).

Duplicating parts of your pictures

Real painters who want to duplicate part of a picture have to do it the hard way – by hand. For computer users, there's no such problem; by using Paint's two powerful selection tools, you can duplicate an item in seconds.

If you've been following the exercises in Word you will have seen how you can use the mouse to select words in a document and then how to copy and paste them as many times as you like. You can do the same with a graphics program such as Microsoft Paint. In Paint, you can select any part of your picture and then delete it, copy it and paste it anywhere you like – you can even paste it into another picture.

Being able to copy parts of your painting and then paste them elsewhere can be a real time saver. Imagine you want to create a picture of a tree with lots of leaves on it. It might take ages to paint all the individual leaves but, if you paint one good one, you can copy and paste it many times all over the tree to create the effect you want.

● Two selection tools

Paint provides two tools to help you select parts of your painting. There's a rectangular one that lets you select simple square or rectangular parts, and there's a free-form tool, with which you can select any shape from your painting.

To use the rectangular selection tool, go to the toolbar at the left of the Paint window and click over the

Paint is a great tool with which to be creative with your PC. Simple designs can become works of art.

top right button (that's the one with a dotted rectangle on it). Return to the painting area and drag with your mouse to select the part of the painting you're interested in.

The advantage of the rectangular Select tool is that it's very quick and easy to use. The downside is that you can only select rectangular areas. However, this is ideal if you want to copy or delete whole items that aren't joined to another part of your picture.

● Free form

To use the Free-Form Select tool, click on the button at the top left of the toolbar – it has a dotted star on it. To use this in the painting area, hold down the left mouse button and drag the tool around the edges of the object you're copying. We show you how to do this in detail on the opposite page.

You can copy any part of a picture by highlighting it and using the Copy and Paste options on the Edit menu.

When you're doing lots of copy and paste actions, remember that keyboard shortcuts can help you work more quickly. When you've selected an area, press [Ctrl]+[C] to copy it, then [Ctrl]+[V] to paste it.

How to make multiple copies

Use Paint's selection tools to cut out repetitive painting and turn one of your paintings into a party invitation. Here we show you how copy and paste works in Paint.

DRAWING A STAR

To draw a star in Paint, use the Polygon tool. This lets you draw straight edges that Paint will form into a solid shape. Select the tool and move the mouse pointer to the painting area. Click and hold down the left mouse button as you drag to draw the first edge. Release the button, move the pointer to the position you want the next corner to be in and click once: Paint will draw the second edge. Repeat this process for each edge until you are back at the start of your first line.

Next, add some extra shapes and fill with colour (see page 69) to create the double-star effect shown in step 1.

1 Here's our star, which we are going to copy and paste (see Drawing a star, left). It is an irregular shape so we'll use the Free-Form Select tool. Choose this by clicking over the top left button on the toolbar.

2 Now go across to the painting area, move the mouse close to the star, click and hold down the left button and start to trace carefully around the outside of the star. As you move the mouse, a black line will appear to show the perimeter of the area.

3 Work your way around the star and try to finish close to your starting point before you release the mouse button. If you don't start and finish at exactly the same point, Paint will wait for you to finish, then tidy things up. Finally, a dotted rectangle will appear around the selected area.

4 Click on the top option of the two colour pictures shown in the lower section of the toolbar, this is called the Opaque option. Then choose Copy from the Edit menu. This makes a copy of the selected part of your picture and puts it in the Windows Clipboard.

5 Before you paste the star, draw a black rectangle to the right of your painting. Now paste a copy of the star by choosing Paste from the Edit menu. Drag and drop this copy of the star over the black area. You'll see that the star's white rectangle surround is also pasted. This is because the Opaque option was selected when we pasted the star from the Clipboard.

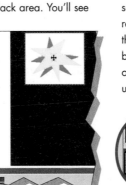

6 Often, it's useful to paste without the surrounding rectangle. To do this, click on the bottom of the two options shown under the toolbar (this is called the Transparent option, below left). Paste and drag the third star over the black area. Because the background colour is white (shown right, in the two colour squares at the left of the colour palette), Paint treats the white area in the pasted copy as transparent.

7 Save time by pasting as many stars as you like on to your invitation. Once you've duplicated an item, you can use Paint's other tools on it. We've used the Flip/Rotate option (left) from the Image menu to rotate each star. We've also changed the colours of the stars using the Fill With Color tool (see pages 64–65). Finally, we added our coloured text (see pages 66–67). On the right is the finished card.

Please come to my party

Your toolbox guide

The key to getting the best from Microsoft Paint is finding out which tools are at your disposal and what you can do with them. Let's dip into the Paint toolbox and review all the 16 available tools to see which are best suited to each job.

If you want to get the most out of Microsoft Paint, it's vital to get to grips with its toolbox. By now, you know what some of the 16 buttons on the toolbox are for and how to use them. Let's take this opportunity to revise what we've already learned and also to fill in the gaps about the other buttons in the toolbox.

On pages 74–75, we saw how the top two buttons select areas of a drawing so that they can be cut from it and pasted somewhere else. The top-left button is the Free-Form Select tool and it allows you to draw freehand around an area to select it. This takes a steady hand to master, but there's always the quicker and easier (if less precise) normal Select tool which you can access from the top-right button on the toolbox. This allows you to select rectangular areas of your drawing.

● **In the second row**
The two buttons on the second row of the toolbox are the Eraser tool and the Fill With Color tool. You can use the Eraser to rub out parts of your drawing and you can choose different sizes for the tool to suit the amount of rubbing out needed.

The Fill With Color tool lets you flood an enclosed area with the currently selected painting colour.

The third row of buttons consists of the Pick Color tool and the Magnifier tool. The first one allows you to pick up the colour of any part of your drawing and make it the currently selected colour.

The Magnifier lets you zoom in on any part of your drawing to see fine details and choose different levels of magnification to suit your needs.

● **Drawing freehand lines**
The Pencil and Brush tools are on the fourth row. These tools provide different styles for drawing freehand lines. A Pencil line is always only one pixel wide, but you can choose a variety of widths and shapes with the Brush.

The Airbrush tool on the fifth row gives you another way of freehand painting on your drawing and offers three different sizes of airbrush.

Next to it is the Text tool, which lets you include text in a variety of sizes, fonts and weights.

● **Shapes and lines**
The sixth row holds the related Line and Curve tools. Line is used to draw straight lines while Curve lets you include smooth curves as part of your drawing.

The last two rows provide you with tools to draw a variety of shapes. The buttons on the seventh row let you draw rectangles and other polygons. The eighth row has tools to draw ellipses and rectangles with rounded corners.

Most of the tools found in a conventional artist's bag are also to be found in the Paint toolbox.

SHORT CUTS

When working close-up on a Paint drawing you often want to see as much of the drawing as possible, so hide the Paint toolbox from view by pressing the [Ctrl] and [T] keys. When you want to see the toolbox again, just press the same two keys.

Microsoft®Paint

Get to know your Paint tools

① The Free-Form Select tool lets you draw around areas of your picture to select them. Then you can cut, copy and paste them somewhere else.

② The normal Select tool lets you select rectangular areas of your drawing. Then you can cut the areas or copy and paste them to another position.

③ The Eraser tool lets you rub out parts of a drawing. You can choose the size of this tool by clicking over one of the shapes shown below the toolbox.

④ The Fill With Color tool allows you to fill an area already filled with a colour (or indeed no colour at all) with another colour of your choice.

⑤ The Pick Color tool lets you select a colour from within your drawing to be the current drawing colour. This is helpful for getting exact colour matches.

⑥ The Magnifier tool lets you zoom in on a selected area of your drawing. You can choose the level of magnification from the options below the toolbox.

⑦ The Pencil tool allows you to draw freehand lines exactly one pixel wide. You can choose the colour you want to draw in from the Paint palette.

⑧ The Brush tool lets you draw freehand lines with a brush effect. You can choose the style and size of brush from the options shown below the toolbox.

⑨ The Airbrush tool allows you to paint areas with an airbrush effect. You can choose the size of this tool from the three offered below the toolbox.

⑩ The Text tool lets you type text into your drawing. You can choose the size, weight and font of the words you type.

⑪ The Line tool allows you to draw straight lines in the currently selected drawing colour. You can choose the width of line you want from the ones shown below the toolbox.

⑫ The Curve tool allows you to draw curves in the currently selected drawing colour.

⑬ The Rectangle tool lets you draw rectangles and squares. You can choose whether the shape is filled or just an outline from the options available below the toolbox. The Rounded Rectangle **⑯** is used in the same way if you want to have rounded corners on the shapes.

⑭ The Polygon tool lets you draw freehand polygons like these complex shapes. You can choose if the polygon is filled in or is just an outline by selecting one of the options below the toolbox.

⑮ The Ellipse tool lets you draw ellipses and circles. You can choose whether it is filled with colour or is just in outline.

Special effects in Paint

Paint has more to offer than the functions available via the toolbox. Here's how to exploit a group of easy-to-use special effects hidden away in one of Paint's menus.

Practice will help you become familiar with the tools offered in Paint and as you get used to using this software, you'll discover that it has hidden depths. You'll develop your own quick ways to achieve the results you want.

However, there's one really useful set of functions you won't find if you only ever use the toolbox. Hidden away in the Image menu are several effects that you can apply to achieve even more creative drawings. Using these different text effects and illustrations will inject a little bit more pizzazz into your personal letters and invitations.

By default, Paint applies these special effects to the whole drawing when you use them. However, you can use the Select and Free-Form Select tools to specify particular areas of your drawing where you want the special effects to be applied. For example, you can use these effects to modify text or even just a single letter in a sentence, as well as to alter shapes or objects in your drawing.

● Types of special effects

There are two main types of special effects you can achieve. Firstly, the Flip/Rotate option in the Image menu gives you the power to rotate your drawing (or a selected part of it) through 90, 180 or 270 degrees, or to flip it horizontally or vertically. Secondly, you can stretch or skew your drawing (or a selected part of it) by using the Stretch/Skew option in the Image menu.

A special dialog box will appear if you choose Flip/Rotate from the Image menu. Here you can simply click over the appropriate button to choose whether you want to flip your drawing horizontally, flip it vertically or rotate it. If you choose the rotation option, then you have the further choice of angle from 90, 180 or 270 degrees. Once you've chosen the effect you want, click the OK button and wait to see the results.

● Stretch and Skew

Similarly, another special dialog box will appear if you choose the Stretch/Skew option. This time it offers you the choice of four effects: horizontal stretch, vertical stretch, horizontal skew or vertical skew. Simply click over the appropriate button for the effect you want. If you choose a stretch, you can type in the percentage by which you want to stretch your drawing; if you choose a skew, you can type in the angle to which you want your drawing skewed.

WHAT IT MEANS

DEFAULT
This word describes the options or settings that your computer programs will use unless you choose something different. For example, Microsoft Word will always use the Times New Roman typeface by default when you start a new document.

Create various eye-catching designs for your cards and letters by using Paint's Stretch and Skew options.

Microsoft® Paint

Special effects with the Image menu

The tools in Paint's Image menu allow you to create some interesting effects with text and basic graphics – perfect for adding a little sparkle to your text documents, invitations and business cards.

1 Let's start by typing in some sample red text. With the left mouse button, select red as the foreground colour from the palette at the bottom left of the screen. Click over the Text tool in the toolbox and draw a text box. Type in some words.

2 Let's see what happens when we stretch the words. Select Stretch/Skew from the Image menu. In the dialog box that appears, type '400' into the vertical percentage box and click on the OK button. After a short wait, you'll see the finished effect (see below, inset).

3 To add a skew effect to the text, select the text with the Select tool and then Stretch/Skew from the Image menu. Type '30' into the Horizontal degrees box in the Skew section and click OK. The result will appear (below, inset).

4 You can also type in negative numbers for the skew effect to achieve a 'reverse' italic image. Use the Text tool to create some new plain text and type '–30' into the Horizontal degrees box in the Skew section.

5 When you press the OK button, the Paint program slants the text from the upper left to lower right. You can apply the same principle to skewing parts of your picture vertically and skew the elements either to the left or to the right. Experiment to see the effects you can get.

6 Now let's combine some effects on shapes and text. Set yellow as the foreground colour and use the Ellipse tool to draw an outline shape. Then use the Fill With Color tool to fill it with yellow. Next, select the shape with the Select tool and use Stretch/Skew from the Image menu. Apply a 45 degrees horizontal skew.

7 Make red the foreground colour, type in some words and then use the Select tool to select a rectangular area around them. Next, choose Stretch/Skew from the Image menu and this time apply a vertical skew to the selected area – we've used one of 42 degrees.

8 Notice that a rectangular area around the skewed text is still selected, but its dimensions have changed. The final step is to move this area over the yellow ellipse, so click somewhere inside the rectangle, hold down the left mouse button and drag and drop the text to position it accurately.

Designing a Christmas card

Creating images can be quick and easy on your PC. With the help of Microsoft Paint and a little practice, you can create stylish designs for anything from labels to greetings cards.

In the step-by-step exercises on pages 64–79, you have learned how to use some of the most important Paint commands and tricks, as well as the tools in the toolbox. Now, by simply combining all that you have learned, it's possible to produce smart-looking pictures. To start, we will show you how to produce an attractive Christmas card cover.

A little planning before you begin will make your task easier. First, form in your mind a clear picture of what you want to draw and then think about how you are going to achieve it. There isn't a specific tool for every job, so you must use lateral thinking to achieve the best results. If you're going to include text, remember to leave space for it on your design. Also, consider the colours

you are going to use. Try to choose colours that will stand out against the background you are using. Some shapes might need to be outlines, so you can use Paint's built-in tools to help you with a lot of the work. Some of the figures might turn out to be quite easy to draw using the Ellipse or Rectangle tool.

● **Drawing something different**

At this point, you might even consider changing parts of your picture if you see an easy way to draw something different. Although you will see examples in the step-by-step guide opposite, don't be afraid to add your own ideas and techniques as you go along.

Making your card

Paint's variety of tools can be used to create all sorts of images. Here we show you how to achieve great results.

1 We need a landscape. It's Christmas, so that means a white ground and blue sky. Choose blue from the colour palette by left-clicking on it. Click the Line tool and draw a line horizontally across the screen. To make sure the line goes right across the page, you will probably have to move the scroll bar to the right. Select the Fill With Color tool (inset) and colour in the top half of the picture.

2 Next, use the Ellipse tool (inset) to draw a snowman's head and body. First, select the colour black from the palette: as you are drawing the snowman on top of a partially white background, you have to ensure he stands out. Next, select the Ellipse tool. Place the cursor where you want his body to start, then drag it across until the circle is big enough. It may take a couple of attempts to get right, so undo your last action to revert to the previous effort if you make a mistake. Use the same method to draw the head on top.

3 Now colour in the snowman. Select white as the foreground colour and fill in the circles. Add some eyes and a mouth by selecting black again and choosing the Brush tool (inset left). Change the brush type to produce a dot wherever you click on the screen (inset right).

4 The next thing to draw is a Christmas tree, using the Polygon tool (inset left). First, select a shade of green as the foreground colour. Next, select the Polygon tool and click the bottom fill option. Decide where the top of your tree is going to be and click and drag the outline of the tree. When you have finished, double-click within your tree and it will be filled in and drawn.

5 To draw snowflakes, use the Text tool and asterisks. Place the cursor where you want a snowflake and click, and the Text toolbar will appear. Select the Times New Roman font, a large font size, such as 26, and type a single asterisk by pressing [Shift] and [8]. It's easiest to create more asterisks by drawing a box around the first asterisk using the Select tool and then using the Copy and Paste commands from the Edit menu to duplicate them. You can also draw snowflakes using the **Wingdings** font.

6 Add a brown rectangle as a tree trunk, then write a greeting using the Text tool (see pages 66–67). Use a solid colour and large text so that it stands out against the snow.

7 The final touch is to add some clouds. For this, the Airbrush tool is ideal. Select the Airbrush tool and choose the largest spray size. Make sure that the foreground colour is white. Spray a shape in the sky to look like a wintry cloud.

8 You can leave the card like this, or spend a little more time adding some extra details, such as a star for the tree, a scarf and hat for the snowman, and some Christmas baubles using the Pencil, Polygon and Ellipse tools. Have fun and don't be afraid to experiment!

MERRY CHRISTMAS

Choosing new colours

At first sight it may appear that Microsoft Paint allows you to choose only a few colours with which to draw pictures. However, you can add many more shades by creating your own customized colours.

W hile working with Paint, you might find that you feel a little restricted by the choice of colours available, as there are only 28 colours in the colour palette shown at the bottom of the screen.

For simple pictures, these colours are adequate to get your ideas across. They cover all the main options – reds, yellows, blues and so on. They are very useful for bold graphics and cartoon-style images with lots of contrast. However, as there are few shades of the same colour, subtle shading effects are not possible.

● Palette picker
Fortunately, Paint provides you with a way to choose any colour you like. Paint's Edit Colors dialog box lets you change an existing palette colour to any other colour you wish. While there are various ways to specify new colours, the best method for those with only a little experience of graphics packages is to

choose new colours by pointing and clicking on the screen. The Edit Colors dialog box provides a large multi-coloured square. You just click on the square on a colour you want and then click on a button to add it to your own custom colour palette. Once you have created your new colour palette, you can use it in any of your other paintings.

● Dotty display
When you choose and customize colours, you might find that some of them appear to be 'dotted'. This is called 'dithering' and occurs when Windows cannot show the true colour you have chosen. The way to avoid dithered colours is to run your computer screen in 'true colour'. This is a mode that shows all colours without any dithering at all. You can choose this mode from the Display Properties window, which is accessed by right-clicking on the Desktop and choosing Properties from the menu that appears.

WHAT IT MEANS

DITHERING
By using two colour combinations, Windows can simulate a third, intermediate colour. This process, called dithering, is often required when you are using the computer while it is running in 256-colour mode.

When working on graphics, dithering is distracting. The solution is to change to true colour mode (we will cover this in detail later in the course).

Custom colours

Pick and choose, from reds to blues and any colour in between, to make your own shades and tones.

CREATING YOUR own customized colours can be extremely handy when you need to work with several different shades of one colour. For example, it would be particularly useful if you wanted to draw a realistic sky, graduating from white through to pale blue and then a darker blue, or perhaps a grass background with varying shades of green. In the example shown below, we'll be choosing colours with which to draw a simple sea and sky. They will change from a mid-blue at the bottom of the picture to a dark blue at the top.

1 Open Paint and double-click anywhere on the colour palette to make the Edit Colors window appear.

2 Click on the Define Custom Colors button. You'll now see a window with a rainbow of colours displayed. From here, you can pick a specific colour from anywhere in the spectrum (inset). The numbers below the main window relate to the colour currently selected.

PC TIPS

If you want to use lots of colours in Paint, you will need to instruct Windows to display the highest number of colours possible. In 256-colour mode, you can see a lot of dithering of colours, while in 24-bit true colour mode all the colours are displayed without any dithering at all. (Note that on some computers 24-bit colour is called 32-bit colour.)

The colours in the box above are dithered in 256 colours; the same colours in 24-bit true colour mode shown in the box below look fine.

3 The first colour we want is a mid-blue. Move the cursor into the blue area of the window. Then move it to the top middle of the blue so that you select a bright blue colour. The colour you choose will be shown in the Color/Solid box. A range of colours, both lighter and darker, will also be shown in the vertical band to the right of the colour window, arranged around the shade you have selected.

4 Click on the Add to Custom Colors button. This will move the colour in the Color/Solid box into the Custom colors palette.

5 It is worth setting all the shades of one particular colour at a time. By doing this, you will be able to compare shades as you go along. Click on an empty box in the Custom colors grid where the next colour can go.

6 Now click in the same area of blue, but this time select a visibly darker shade. This is done by clicking on the tall, thin shaded band to the right of the large colour square. When you have found the shade that you want, click on Add to Custom Colors.

7 Repeat this process and continue to select further shades of your chosen colour until you have at least six progressively darker shades stored in the Custom colors palette.

8 You can now add your new shades of blue to a drawing that requires them. Even a simple picture will often benefit from using a range of subtle custom shades that would not be possible using Paint's standard palette.

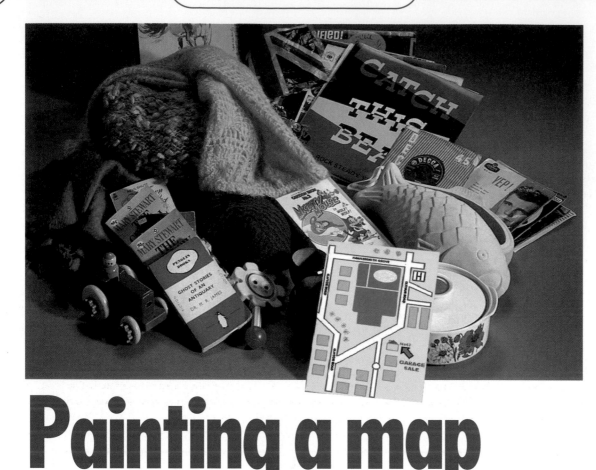

Now you've mastered the basics of Microsoft Paint, there are all sorts of practical uses for your new skills. For instance, here's how you can quickly create a simple and effective map showing directions to a jumble sale.

Painting a map

You should by now be familiar with how to use all the tools on Microsoft Paint's toolbar (see pages 76–77), as well as the more advanced features hidden away in its menus (see pages 78–79). The only limit on how creative you can be is your own imagination – all it takes is a little patience and practice.

For example, let's imagine you've volunteered to do the publicity leaflets for a jumble sale at the village hall. The text part of the leaflet is straightforward and can easily be created in a Microsoft Word document. However, you now need to add some directions about how to get to the jumble sale. The best way is to provide a map, so let's make an attempt at this by using Paint. Remember, we'll be able to take the finished Paint map and insert it into our Word document (see PC Tips, right).

● **Combination of Paint skills**

Drawing a map requires a combination of Paint tools and skills (see opposite, Creating a simple map). If you're not quite sure where to start, it might be a good idea to make a rough pencil and paper sketch to work from.

The first thing to do in Paint is to use the Pencil tool to sketch in the roads freehand –

it doesn't matter if your mouse control is a bit shaky at first, you can always start again from the beginning. A good tip is to save your map each time you complete a correct stage of drawing it. Then, if you make a mistake, you can just close your document without saving it and reopen the last version you did save.

Once the roads are finished, it's easy to include buildings by using the Rectangle tool. Other elements (such as the duck pond we use in our example) can be added by using the Rectangle, Ellipse, Rounded Rectangle and Polygon tools. A neat way to include features such as churches or telephone boxes is to use the Text tool to add symbols from unusual Windows fonts, such as Wingdings (see page 81). The Fill With Color and Airbrush tools are really handy for including countryside features, for example, trees, bushes and fields.

The last stage is to use the Text tool to label all the important landmarks on the map. Don't be restricted to adding horizontal text, as there's a clever way of including vertical text: use the Flip/Rotate option in the Image menu to rotate your map. Then you can add a text label and rotate the map back to its original position.

PC TIPS

You can include Paint drawings in Microsoft Word documents (see pages 46–49). Use the Select tool in Paint to choose part of your drawing, then select Copy from the Edit menu.

Switch to Word and paste from the Edit menu to insert the selected part of the drawing into your Word document.

Creating a simple map

You can use all your accumulated knowledge of Paint to create a variety of useful graphics. Here's how to draw a map showing the directions to a village jumble sale.

1 The first thing to do is sketch in the roads. Click on the Pencil tool in the toolbar, choose black from the palette and use the drag and drop technique to draw in the roads. We can use the Rectangle tool to add some buildings to our map. Click on the Rectangle tool button in the toolbar, choose the middle option from below the toolbar and select black as the foreground colour and orange as the background colour. Now just use your mouse to draw the required building shapes.

2 The next step is to add the duck pond. Keep black as the foreground colour and choose blue as the new background colour from the palette. Then click on the Ellipse button in the toolbar and use your mouse to add the pond.

3 Now we want to fill in a green area to denote the school playing field. We do this by first using the Line tool to draw a line between the loop in the road. Then we select the Fill With Color tool and choose green as the foreground colour, clicking on the area we want to fill.

4 Next let's mark the position of the church with a cross. Select the Text tool and click where you want the church to be. If the Text toolbar doesn't appear, go to the View menu and select Text Toolbar. Then set 36pt Wingdings (see page 81) as the font and type a capital V to get a cross character.

5 Don't forget the bushes beside the duck pond! Select green as the foreground colour from the palette and click over the Airbrush button in the toolbar. Pick the largest spray area from the options and paint in the bushes by holding down the button and moving the mouse around.

6 Now we're ready to start labelling the map's key features. Choose black as the foreground colour in the palette, click over the Text button in the toolbar, choose a legible font, such as 12pt Times New Roman, and draw the box where you want your first label to go.

7 We have to label the playing fields vertically, so choose Flip/Rotate from the Image menu and rotate your map through 90 degrees. Pick white as the foreground colour and use the Text tool to add the label.

8 The final touch is to put the map back round the right way. Select Flip/Rotate again from the Image menu and this time rotate your map through 270 degrees.

Know Paint's limits

Microsoft Paint offers a quick and easy way of creating simple graphics, such as party invitations, maps and logos. But this program does have its limitations.

P aint is a pixel-based painting program. This means that whenever you use its tools to create a picture, you are actually painting areas composed of individual dots (or pixels) in a new colour. So, for example, if you use Paint's Pencil tool to draw a straight black line, you are really just changing the colour of the pixels that make up the line to black.

This method of creating graphics by editing pixels is called **bitmap** painting and Paint is one of the best-known examples of a bitmap painting program. However, while programs like Paint are simple to use, they have limitations when it comes to creating more complicated graphics.

The first limitation of Paint is that once you've drawn something, the only way to modify it later is to change its pixels by drawing over them with something new.

For example, if you draw a filled red rectangle and want to come back later and change it to an unfilled rectangle with a blue outline, the only way to do it is by painting over the original drawing. It's just as awkward to change other aspects of the rectangle, such as its height and width.

● No object

These difficulties occur because any object you draw in Paint isn't stored as an object – it's simply an area of coloured pixels. This limitation is more serious than it first appears. Here are some examples of the things you can't do because of it: you can't go back and change the typeface or size of any text in your picture; you can't go back and change the width of a line; and you can't go back and change a filled circle to an outline one.

We've also seen that you can move items around a Paint drawing using the various selection tools. The problem is that these tools only select an area of painted pixels rather than the objects themselves. This becomes a serious problem when you have items that overlap in a drawing. For example, if you have a square that overlaps a circle, you can't select the square and move it to reveal the circle behind. Another limitation of bitmap drawings becomes apparent when you try to enlarge them. What may look like a smooth line on your original drawing will turn into an ugly line full of jagged edges (also called 'jaggies') when you try to make it bigger.

The more you enlarge a bitmap image, the more jagged the edges become. This is one of the main limitations of a pixel-based painting program, such as Microsoft Paint.

Bitmaps versus vectors

For pictures unsuitable for bitmap painting programs, another type of graphics software is available. These programs are called drawing – or vector graphics – programs.

PAINT ALLOWS YOU to save your pictures in bitmap form only. There are, however, more sophisticated graphics programs – known as vector graphics programs – that overcome the main limitations of bitmaps (see below). For example, you can change any aspect of drawn objects, such as their width, outline and colour, at any time because they are stored in the image as individual objects. In addition, these objects suffer no loss of quality or smoothness if you want to enlarge them. However, the extra sophistication of vector graphics programs means that they are harder to use. A bitmap painting package is the ideal choice for simple graphics, but for anything more ambitious, a drawing program is worth the effort.

In the next volume of *PCs made easy* we begin a step-by-step course for a vector graphics program – CorelDRAW.

1 Here is a Paint picture with three overlapping items: a green circle, a blue rectangle and a thick red line. Like most bitmap painting programs, Paint makes it easy to draw these things on top of each other, but remember we are really painting pixels rather than drawing objects.

2 As we've seen before in our Paint exercises, we can use the Select tool to select a rectangular region that contains the circle, rectangle and line. Then we can use the mouse to drag and drop them (as if they were a single item) to a new position in our drawing.

3 But what happens if we want to move the blue rectangle to a new position? If we use the Select tool we can choose a region that matches the area occupied by the rectangle. Let's see what happens when we try to move it to a new position.

4 Now there's a problem: the Select tool only allows us to select an area of painted pixels, not a proper object. The trouble is that the selected area includes a portion of the red line and, because the green circle has been painted over, there's a hole where the rectangle used to be. The only way to get the drawing you want is to start another Paint drawing.

VECTOR DRAWING PROGRAMS

The key difference between a bitmap painting program and a vector drawing program is that the latter stores each item of a drawing as an individual object. You can select such an object simply by clicking over it and change its properties at any time. So, for instance, you can change the colour, size and angle of rotation and many other aspects of an object. It's also easy to pick up an object and move it to another location in the drawing without harming any other objects which it may happen to overlap (shown right and above).

In fact, all the objects in a vector drawing program are stored as mathematical formulae by the program. The advantage of this is that if you change the size of the objects, they retain their smoothness. You can also alter a vector graphics object (by, for example, stretching or twisting it) and it will retain its smoothness.

Hardware

The Multimedia PC

You've bought your computer and set it up. But what are the parts that make up a PC?

Your home PC is a great example of evolution in action. From origins as a silent office computer, it has evolved into a magnificent all-singing, all-dancing Multimedia system.

The main reason for its success is that no matter what you want to do with your PC, you can adapt it to take on completely new tasks. Your home PC shares perhaps 80 per cent of its components with today's business PC, but with the addition of just a handful of extras, it plays music CDs, shows DVD movies and paints and prints stunning colour pictures.

● Mix and match

Each PC component is replaceable and that makes it easy to change one component for another. You can usually mix and match components from different PC makers, and that increases your options hugely. There are literally thousands of items to choose from.

For example, if you want your PC to go faster, you can often swap its processor for a faster one. Imagine being able to change a Ford's engine to one from a Ferrari!

Swapping components is only half the story; your PC can also grow to take on advances in technology that were hardly dreamt of when the US

Keyboard

The keyboard allows you to type documents and input instructions that tell your PC what to do. It inherited its 'QWERTY' layout from the typewriter and has over 100 keys which give all the options you need to make the most of your PC's power and versatility.

Monitor

It might look like a TV screen, but in fact your monitor is much more powerful. Both can show full colour images, but your monitor can show pictures and text in much finer detail.

Speakers

All PCs can produce stereo sound using simple desktop speakers, but a state-of-the-art Multimedia PC has surround sound speakers to make the most of movie soundtracks and game sound effects.

DVD/CD-ROM drives

PCs use CDs and DVDs which both have high capacity. You can play music CDs and install software from data CDs on any PC with a CD-ROM drive. Many PCs have a DVD-ROM drive which can read CDs as well as DVDs. The drive is part of the system unit, see page 92.

Floppy disk drive

Floppy disks store only a small amount of data, and they are best used for transferring small files from one PC to another. The drive is part of the system unit, which is covered in more detail on page 92.

Mouse

The mouse is essential for moving efficiently around the computer screen – as you move the mouse the pointer moves on screen.
A mouse usually has two buttons, although a few have three and some only one.

computer firm IBM first created the PC in the early 1980s.

Speakers, DVD and CD-ROM drives, digital cameras and even video cameras are already part of the Multimedia experience. As well as making PCs more fun for home users, these expansion devices also make PCs capable of completely new jobs. It's possible to record movies on to the hard disk of your computer, edit them, add special effects, then record them back on to video tape. The possibilities today are enormous.

● **Around the Multimedia PC**

With all these replaceable and expandable components, your Multimedia PC might seem like a confusing collection of boxes and wires. It can be hard work to figure out what does what and why.

In this tour around the Multimedia PC, we'll show you how it all works together in harmony. We'll also lift the lid and take a look at what goes on inside the system unit itself. Knowing how the sum of the parts fits together is a great way to begin to get more from the whole.

Outside...

These components allow you to enter information into your PC, display what comes out and have more fun with games.

Printer

For home PC users, the ideal printer is the colour inkjet (left), which can print colour pictures and newsletters as well as traditional black and white letters. Laser printers (above) provide the best black and white printing quality.

MP3 player

You can create and download MP3 files from your PC to one of these portable devices to listen to music on the move. They use computer memory chips instead of tape so they're compact and never skip – even if you're jogging.

Digital camera

Digital photography cuts out film-processing costs and lets you see and edit your photos on the computer screen within minutes of taking them. All you need is a digital camera, which connects to the sockets on the back of the PC.

Microphone

With a Multimedia PC you can record your voice and sound effects on to your computer. The microphone connects to the sound card, which converts the sound waves into numbers that the computer can store and replay at any time through the speakers.

Game controller

Many PC games are a lot easier to master and a lot more realistic with the right input device. A joystick or steering wheel plugs into the PC and works just like the controls in a jet fighter and Formula 1 car. Some devices use feedback, making the wheel wobble in your hand as you turn a tight corner.

Mouse mat

It's a low-tech component, but don't forget it. A mouse mat makes your mouse easier to move and prolongs its working life (see page 93).

...and inside

If you understand the various component parts that have gone into producing your PC, you will have a much better idea of what you can get it to do.

System unit

The system unit is the most important part of the PC; inside are its 'brains'. Everything connects to the system unit – its back panel has sockets for all the external components shown on page 91. Some PCs have an all-in-one monitor and system unit.

Processor

This is the true brain of the PC and the most important component on the motherboard. It processes, understands and acts on the instructions contained in your software programs. Processors operate at speeds of several millions of instructions per second.

Memory

Every PC uses memory – special chips on the motherboard – as a high speed workspace for the processor's calculations. When you start a program or open a letter, it is copied from the hard disk into the memory where the processor can work on it quickly. The more memory you have, the faster your PC will run. Memory is often referred to as **RAM.**

Graphics card

The graphics card (sometimes called the video card) shows on the screen the image that the processor has created in the memory. Sometimes the graphics card is built on to the motherboard, but often it's a separate expansion card (see Motherboard).

Hard disk drive

Your PC needs somewhere to store long-term information because its memory literally goes blank when the PC is switched off. The hard disk provides a huge storage area for programs and documents that lasts as long as you want – even when the PC is turned off. The disk sits in an airtight metal box.

Motherboard

This is your PC's largest circuit board. All the internal components are either on the motherboard or connected to it. It has a bank of slots where you can plug in expansion cards, which are extra circuit boards that allow your PC to perform new tasks.

WHAT IT MEANS

RAM

RAM stands for Random Access Memory, although in practical terms it means memory that can be both read from and written to. This contrasts with Read Only Memory – ROM – from which you can read information, but not write to it.

Sound and modem cards

Most PCs have an expansion card to play sounds through the PC's speakers and another card, called a modem, which adapts computer data so that it can be transmitted over a telephone line. Some PCs use an external modem, which plugs into the back of the PC.

Maintaining your mouse

Spare a thought for your hardworking mouse as you scroll around the Desktop. It takes a lot of punishment, but keep it clean and you'll be able to point with precision for a long time.

THE MOUSE is the main way you move around the computer screen. You use it to pick up and move files around the Desktop, scroll through documents, perform program commands and click on 'hotlinks' in Internet sites. Together with your keyboard, your mouse is a crucial way of communicating with your computer and therefore deserves some basic care.

Like any small device with moving parts, the mouse may not last forever. It is simple and inexpensive to replace your mouse if it does suffer a fatal accident, but with sensible use and simple maintenance its working life can be greatly extended. Not all mice use ball and rollers; some modern devices have no moving parts and need no internal cleaning at all.

Your mouse will become 'sticky' as it picks up dirt during use. Make sure your PC is switched off before tackling your dirty mouse. There's no need to unplug the mouse from the computer, but this may make the process easier.

1 To remove surface grease and dirt, rub a mouse wipe gently but firmly all over the mouse's top and underside.

2 To clean the moveable parts of the mouse, turn the mouse over and twist the circular panel anti-clockwise a quarter turn.

3 When the panel is removed, turn the mouse over and the ball will fall out (hopefully into your hand).

4 Clean the mouse ball first. Take a clean mouse wipe and, using the tips of your fingers and thumb, firmly rub the surface of the ball. The special wipes contain a solvent to help break down any dirt. You'll be amazed at the dirt that comes off the mouse ball.

5 The biggest problems arise from the build-up of grime on the mouse's three internal rollers. Scrape the dirt from each of the rollers using a matchstick. Make sure that you remove all the dirt or you may find the mouse's movements are uneven when you use it again.

6 Reassemble the mouse by popping the ball back into the cavity and refitting the mouse panel. You'll get the most from your mouse if you clean it regularly. Keeping the area around your PC clean and using a mouse mat will reduce the amount of cleaning needed.

A tour around your keyboard

Shortcuts and hidden functions are just two of the secrets of your computer's keyboard. Find out more in this quick guided tour.

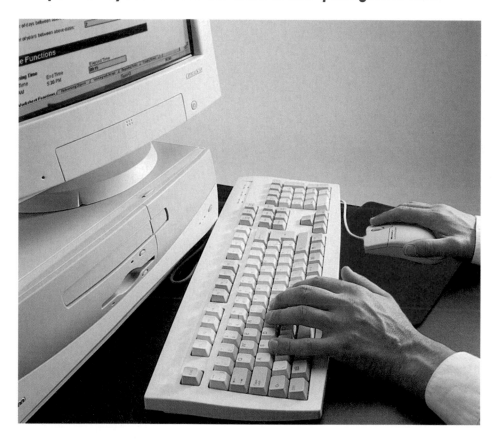

The PC keyboard, with its 100 or so keys, is taken for granted by most people without a thought as to how it works, how it can be used more efficiently and how to look after it. Knowing all these things about your keyboard will help you get more from your home computing.

The heart of the keyboard is based on the typewriter layout that even two-finger typists recognize. However, in addition to the normal keys found on a typewriter, there is a numeric keypad that looks more like a calculator keyboard. This is useful when you type in lots of numbers.

How well do you know your keyboard? Realize your PC's maximum potential by taking a little time to understand the keyboard's lesser-known keys.

Don't let the missing multiply and divide signs catch you out – computers use [*] for multiply and [/] for divide. These are usually the middle two keys on the top row of the numeric key pad.

● Hit the right key
When you press a key, three things happen. The initial press of the key pushes two metal strips together to form an electrical connection. This tells the computer which key has

been pressed. Then a spring or flexible membrane under the key returns it to its upright position. Finally, the key makes a 'click' sound so that you know you have successfully pressed it, without having to look at the screen.

● A capital key
The best way of using your keyboard is to learn the shortcuts built into your programs. These will involve multiple key strokes, so you have to press two or three keys at once.

To get the hang of shortcuts, consider how you produce a capital (or upper case) letter in a document. Normally, pressing the [P] key produces a small (lower case) 'p'. To get a capital 'P', you must press [Shift] and [P].

Windows shortcuts use the [Ctrl] and the [Alt] keys, and you use them like the [Shift] key. For example, if you press [Alt]+[F4], the program or window you are using will close. [Ctrl]+[Esc] will bring up the Start menu at the bottom of your screen – even if you can't see the Start button.

Once you're used to shortcuts, you'll find Windows a lot quicker because you don't need to keep moving your hand away from the keyboard to the mouse and back.

CHECKPOINT ✔

KEYBOARD CARE

☑ To clean your keyboard, turn the PC off, then wipe off any dirt with a slightly damp cloth. There might be dust and dirt trapped between the keys, so use a can of compressed air to blow the dust and dirt away.

☑ Keep food and drink away from the keyboard. A spilled drink can quickly render a keyboard useless.

☑ Prevention is better than cure. If, try as you might, you can't keep food and drink away, then use a keyboard seal. This is a plastic cover which protects your keyboard, but still lets you type. When it gets dirty, just pull it off and wash it.

The keys that unlock your PC

Some keys on your keyboard are more useful than you might think and a few of them are not much use at all! Here's what they all do.

① [Esc] The Escape key is most often used to cancel the current menu or dialog box.

② [F1] The first of the function keys is usually used to summon up help in programs.

③ [F2] to [F12] The other function keys send commands to the software you are using to offer quick access to different options.

④ [Delete] and **[Backspace]** Both keys delete a character: [Delete] removes the one to the right of the cursor, [Backspace] removes one to the left.

⑤ The **[Print Screen]**, **[Pause]** and the **[Scroll Lock]** keys (together with the **[Alt Gr]** key to the right of the spacebar) are almost redundant. Designed for 1980s software, they are rarely used by modern Windows programs.

⑥ Numeric keypad This has two functions controlled by the **[Num Lock]** key. When

[Num Lock] is on (indicated by a small light near the top right of the keyboard), the keypad produces numbers and maths symbols. With [Num Lock] turned off, the keypad actions duplicate the cursor keys.

⑦ [Home], [End], [Page Up] and **[Page Down]** These keys move you around your documents quickly.

⑧ Cursor keys These arrow keys move the cursor – the text insertion point in word processors, the cell highlighted in spreadsheets, etc. – around the screen.

⑨ Menu key Found on all but the oldest of keyboards, this brings up the same menu you get by right-clicking the mouse button.

⑩ Windows logo Accesses the Start menu – a few old keyboards lack this key.

⑪ Spacebar Inserts a space between text characters (letters) in your documents.

⑫ [Shift], [Ctrl] and **[Alt]** These keys can be used with other keys to create shortcuts.

⑬ [Tab] This key adds spacing in documents. You can also use it to move around dialog boxes and the Windows Desktop.

The 'QWERTY' keyboard layout was inherited from typewriters. This strange layout was originally designed over a hundred years ago to slow typists down. With other layouts, fast typists could jam the typewriter.

Focus on your monitor

Your monitor can provide a high-quality sharp image, but to avoid straining your eyes, make sure that it's properly adjusted. It's not difficult to achieve a crystal clear image when you know how.

Your monitor – the computer screen – is like a window through which you communicate with the computer. If you use the computer a lot, you may spend hours looking at the screen, so it's vital that it's giving you the best possible picture.

It is very likely that your picture isn't the best it could be, especially if someone else set up the computer and it hasn't been adjusted since. It's often hard to tell if a computer monitor is set correctly, unless you know what to look for. Since a poorly set-up monitor contributes to fatigue and eye strain, a few minutes spent adjusting the image are essential. Adjusting the picture – even cleaning the glass screen – can often make a spectacular improvement, and you should check that your monitor is set up to achieve the best possible picture quality.

● Cleaning

The monitor produces static electricity. That means it attracts fine dust like a magnet, and once the screen has been used for some time, it will have a coating of dust. Even though you can't see it easily, this dust will block the view. It acts to disperse light as it leaves the screen, and this leads to what looks like a fuzzy, or slightly out of focus, image.

● Adjusting picture quality

Modern monitors have a whole host of adjustments, but the most important – and often misunderstood – are the brightness and contrast settings. In addition to making sure that you can see the full range of light and dark detail in the image on your PC's screen, these controls can also affect how sharp the picture looks.

Almost all modern monitors allow you to adjust the image through an

You can get special test software to help you adjust your monitor, but you can do much of the fine-tuning yourself by adjusting the image's brightness and contrast and making sure it fills the full area of the screen.

on-screen menu, which works much like the on-screen adjustments you make with the remote control on a modern TV set (see opposite page).

A few older low-cost monitors used physical dials or knobs, usually tucked away on the bottom edge of the monitor. In both cases, the same set of symbols is used to represent the different settings. For example, the brightness control is represented by a sun icon – a circle with lines radiating from it – and the contrast control by a half filled-in circle.

You should also adjust the size and position of the image: the Windows Desktop should fill as much of the screen as possible. If your Desktop has a large and ugly black border, you can adjust the monitor to stretch the image area to fit the screen.

PC TIPS

Your monitor might have a degauss control. You'll rarely need it but it's necessary if there's a discoloured area on the screen (due to magnetic build-up). Access this control using the screen menu (see opposite) and use it to demagnetize the screen. You'll hear a slight thump and the image will wobble then settle again.

Improving your monitor's picture

Just like a television, your computer monitor has controls to adjust the picture. Make sure that you're treating your eyes to the best possible view by fine-tuning the image quality and its size and position.

1 Modern monitors provide a small set of buttons that allow you to adjust the image via on-screen menus. Look for a set of buttons on the front bezel under the glass screen. On some monitors these buttons reside under a flip-down panel. Although this model has seperate brightness and contrast buttons, we have used the main menu button to make all the adjustments for clarity.

2 Switch your PC on, open up a Word window and fill the document area with some test text. You will use this to help get the best possible settings. Press the menu button on the monitor; check your PC or monitor manual if you are not sure which this is.

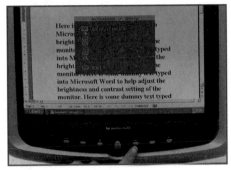

3 The menu's first page appears on the screen. It may not look exactly as shown, but will offer the same controls. Use the buttons on the monitor to select the brightness control; turn it full up. This makes the very edges of the monitor turn from black to slightly grey.

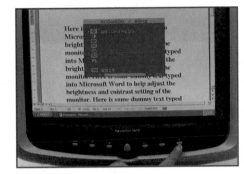

4 Now turn the brightness control down slowly until these grey edges just merge into the monitor's black border. This setting is correct – now only truly black areas in the image are sure to be perfectly black.

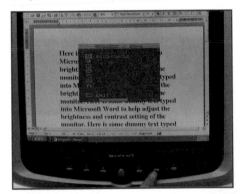

5 Use the menu buttons to select the contrast control and adjust this to set the brightness of the white area of the Word document. If you set it too high, the text may start to look fuzzy – turn it down a little.

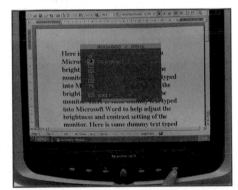

6 Now select the menu's size and position controls. These let you adjust the screen image so that it fills the full area of the screen.

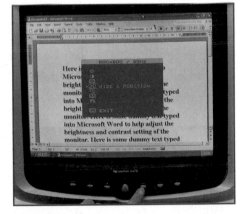

7 The size and position controls often interact, and you may have to tweak one and go back to tweak the other. The aim is to minimize the black border around the Windows Desktop. On many monitors there's a small unused area of glass, but on most you can get very close to the edge of the screen.

PC TIPS

Use a glass-cleaning spray on the screen, making sure the monitor is switched off. Spray a little cleaner on a soft cloth (never on the monitor itself) and wipe the glass. Alternatively use screen wipes, available from computer stores. Make sure that the screen is adjusted to the most comfortable angle on its tilt-and-swivel adjusters. As well as pointing towards you, angle the monitor so it doesn't catch the reflection from a window or a light, as this will make it hard to see the display.

Bits and bytes

Computer equipment – from memory to modems to hard disks – is always measured in bits and bytes. If you've ever wondered what this jargon really means, read on.

From the biggest Internet computers to the smallest palmtop devices, storage space is an important issue. Each and every operating system, program, document and image file requires a certain amount of space, whether it's stored in memory chips, on the hard disk or on a floppy disk or CD.

● **Storing information**

Computer storage is mainly measured in bytes, kilobytes (KB), megabytes (MB) and gigabytes (GB). There are 1024 bytes in a kilobyte, 1024KB in a megabyte and 1024MB in a gigabyte. The table, right, helps to put the numbers in perspective: think of a byte as a single letter (A, B, etc); modern hard disks can store over 20,000,000,000 of them.

Each byte is made up of even tinier units, called bits. These are the most fundamental building blocks, the smallest possible pieces of computer information. Effectively, a bit is like a switch: it can be either on or off. In the binary code that all computers use, this is expressed as either a 1 or a 0 – hence the name bit, which is short for Binary digIT.

A bit is so small that it doesn't mean much on its own. But add it to other bits and the computer sees the combination as a code for a number or letter. Eight bits make a unit of information, one byte.

1KB is roughly equal to half a page of typed text. You can see how adding letters and words to your documents affects file sizes in the exercise on the opposite page.

STORAGE SPACE EXAMPLES

Modern hard disks are so large that you're very unlikely to run out of storage space on your home computer. However, it's helpful to have an idea of the amount of storage required for different types of files and storage devices. The following figures are typical examples:

Alphabet stored in a text file	26 bytes
Alphabet stored in a Word file	20KB
One-page Word letter	22KB
Home budget Excel spreadsheet	50KB
Digital photograph	400KB
Floppy disk capacity	1.44MB
Three-minute MP3 file	3MB
Normal CD-ROM capacity	650MB
Windows folder	900MB

In fact, the Windows operating system and the programs you have installed usually take up most of your hard disk, and it's because of program size that the CD-ROM drive was introduced. CD-ROMs can store large amounts of information – such as interactive encyclopedias – without filling up your hard disk drive.

Only if you have an older PC with a smaller hard disk do you need to worry about storage space. However, it is a good idea to try to keep at least five per cent of space free on your hard disk at all times. We looked at the basics of file management on pages 18–21.

Exploring the size of your documents

Follow these straightforward steps to see the relationship between the amount of information contained in your documents and the amount of hard disk space used to store them.

1 Open the My Documents folder by clicking on the Start menu, then All Programs. Highlight My Documents on the next panel. This will open the My Documents folder.

2 A window pops up to show what's stored in this folder; the exact contents depend on the files and folders you have previously created. Double-click one of the folders that holds Word documents.

3 You can now see the contents of this folder displayed as large icons. Next to each icon is a brief note of the type of file and the file's size. Some files are much bigger than others: the todolist text file is only 1KB whereas the poster document – which contains a space-hungry graphic image – is over 200 times larger.

4 Choose one of the smaller Word documents in your folder and double-click on its icon.

PC TIPS

To check how much hard disk space you have left, access the My Computer folder through the Start menu as in Step 1. Click once on the (C:) icon. The amount of free space is shown in the Details panel on the left of the window.

5 As soon as it opens, select Save As in Word's File menu and save a copy of this document. Call it demo, or something similar. This leaves your original document safe and intact and allows you to work on the demo document.

6 Go to the end of the demo document and type in a page or so of dummy text. You can use the Copy and Paste commands (see pages 16–17) to quickly fill out the page.

7 Save the document and switch back to the view of your folder's contents. Notice that the size of the demo document is now slightly larger than the original document. However, even an extra page of text hasn't added much to the document's size – text is very space efficient.

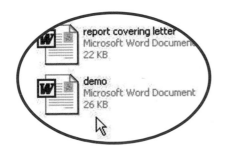

8 In contrast, graphic images take up far more space. Switch back to your demo document and press [Print Screen] on the keyboard to take a snapshot of the Windows screen. Then select Paste from the Edit menu to add the snapshot image to your demo document (see pages16–17).

9 Save the file and then switch back to your folder. Now the document has increased in size considerably. The exact amount will vary depending on the size of your screen and the amount of detail in the graphic.

Adding more memory

Adding more memory is one of the easiest and least expensive upgrades you can make to your computer – and it can also be one of the most effective.

I t's easy to think of your PC as a single box, much like a video recorder or a CD player. However, unlike a video or a CD player – which you tamper with at your peril – a PC is built to be upgradable.

There are two reasons you might want to upgrade your computer: to add new functions and capabilities (adding a larger monitor or plugging in a scanner, for example) or to make your PC work faster.

● Upgrading for performance
It's a fact of computing life that once you've bought a PC, newer, faster models will hit the shops within months. It's also true that new software often works more slowly than previous versions because of all its new features. It's not unusual to

find that upgrading your software seems to make your computer run slower! To counter this performance problem, you can change or add individual components inside your computer. For example, changing to a better graphics card will make the software that uses it run faster. Without a doubt though, the best way to make your computer run much

faster is to add more Random Access Memory (RAM) – and in all cases, the more the merrier.

● More memory
Windows likes memory – the more you've got, the more easily Windows can make space for the huge number of programs and files it uses. Just a year or so ago, very few home PC's were sold with more than 64MB of RAM which seemed plenty – it's enough to store 67,108,864 bytes (see pages 98–99).

However, many programs (including Windows) can use up many millions of bytes. When Windows runs out of memory for the programs and documents it is using, it stores them temporarily on the hard disk. You might notice your computer's hard disk light flashing from time to time, even when you're not opening or saving programs or documents on the hard disk. This is a sign that Windows is swapping information between the memory and the computer's hard disk.

Unfortunately, the hard disk is much slower than the RAM memory

With each version of Windows, Microsoft has increased the amount of RAM required to run it. Windows XP requires at least 128MB – more than 30 times as much as Windows 95.

Windows 95							
Windows 98							
Windows Me							
Windows XP							
0	4	8	16	32	64	128	256

MB

WHAT IT MEANS

DIMM

A Dual inline memory module is a tiny circuit board containing memory chips. It plugs into matching slots on the PC's motherboard. Most PCs use DIMMs, although a few very fast PCs use other types of memory. Your PC's manual should tell you which your PC uses.

and swapping the information from one to the other is also a slow process. With more memory – 128MB or even 256MB – Windows has to do much less of this swapping, and as a result its programs run more quickly and smoothly.

● Memory costs

Memory is the most cost-effective upgrade you can buy. While Windows XP can just about run on a PC with 64MB, adding another 64MB significantly boosts performance,

RAM memory comes in strips called DIMMs and is simple to install, but it is fragile and should be handled only by an experienced technician.

and costs as little as £20. However, due to the volatile nature of the computer business, the price is subject to fluctuation.

As memory is supplied on **DIMM** modules, adding memory is a simple, and therefore cheap, upgrade. Since computers normally have several slots for memory modules, you can sometimes add more without replacing your existing modules. However, it's still worth getting a dealer or computer expert to advise on memory purchase and to install the new DIMMs, as it's important to get exactly the right type (see Fitting the right type of memory, below).

Try to track down a local dealer who either builds systems or does repairs – he may charge a little more for the memory than the big mail order firms that advertise in the magazines, but he will probably fit it free of charge.

How much memory you can add depends on how many free memory module slots there are on the motherboard. Some older PCs may have motherboards with two types of memory slots: DIMM slots and an obsolete type known as single inline memory modules, or SIMMs. The latter are best ignored.

Although the very fastest new PCs use special memory slots (see Fitting the right type of memory, below), most use DIMM slots, typically two or three. One of the main advantages of DIMMs is that they can be added

singly. So if your PC has two 32MB DIMMs and one spare DIMM slot you can add another 64MB DIMM to take the total RAM up to 128MB.

● No software installation

One of the best aspects of adding more memory compared to other computer add-ons is that there's no extra software to install or set up after the new memory has been added. Windows uses the extra memory straight away so that each and every one of your programs can work more efficiently.

Here we can see two vacant slots for memory modules on the motherboard.

Here are the same two slots with two 64MB memory modules fitted in position.

FITTING THE RIGHT TYPE OF MEMORY

We don't recommend that you try fitting new RAM yourself, even if you like the idea of opening up your PC 'box' and looking around inside. The actual fitting isn't difficult, as long as you are careful and dexterous, but it is possible to cause irreparable damage, for example, it's all too easy to destroy memory chips with static electricity.

It's also easy to get the wrong kind of memory module – and once you've opened the sealed pack, the supplier won't change it. There is a vast array of different types of memory and this can be very confusing. Fitting the wrong kind of memory module could damage the memory, your computer – or both.

You will see many abbreviations used in adverts: RD-RAM, DDR, SDRAM, PC100 and so on. You might also see references to parity and non-parity. All this jargon refers to the various different ways that the memory chips work.

SDRAM chips are the latest type of chips and are commonly used in PCs that use DIMM slots. Despite the fact that these chips are new, the fast pace of PC development means that there are several different variants. These subtle variations are based on the speed at which the PC's motherboard operates.

For example, for motherboards that run at 100MHz, 100MHz DIMMs (known as PC100 DIMMs) are required. Similarly, motherboards running at 133MHz need matching DIMMs (known as PC133 DIMMs). Some newer Pentium 4 PCs use RD-RAM, and a few use DDR. Both are potentially faster than SDRAM, but still fairly rare. In general, the faster and newer the technology, the more expensive the memory modules are to buy. Your computer's manual should tell you which types of memory your computer can work with, but a computer dealer will be better able to check the type your computer is fitted with and, if necessary, fit a similar type.

Choosing a printer

Printers are important pieces of hardware – they let you see the documents you have created on paper. You can then check your work and print out as many copies as you need. As with other PC accessories, the right choice of printer depends on what you want to use it for.

In the past, PC users had little choice when it came to printers. Nowadays, there are scores to choose from, and the prices vary considerably. At the bottom of the printer cost range are low-cost but slow colour inkjet printers. At the top are professional laser printers giving pin-sharp printouts in full colour. In between, there is a range of options, but unless you're working on a tight budget, the choice you have to make is between a colour inkjet printer designed for the home market or a laser printer for quality black-and-white work.

● A question of quality

Although colour inkjet printers can be sluggish and not give pin-sharp print, they can turn out dazzling posters, photographs and letters in full colour, making them ideal for family use. Moderately priced laser printers, on the other hand, give only black and white, but are quick and produce top-quality

printouts, making them ideal for anyone running a business from home. Let's have a look at these two types of printer.

● Inkjet printers

Recent advances in inkjet printing technology mean that quality full-colour printing is now within the reach of every home PC user. Inkjet printers work by heating ink in the print head so that a bubble forms and forces an ink droplet out of a nozzle – the inkjet. Some use a piezoelectric 'pump' instead, but the effect is the same – to force a jet of ink out onto the paper. The nozzle has to be very fine – finer even than

A colour inkjet is the best all-round family choice unless you also need a printer to run a business from home.

a human hair – to produce the detail needed for quality printing.

There is one set of jets for each of the different coloured inks. Strangely, the colour is made by using inks of just three colours: cyan (a kind of bluey-green), magenta (purply-red) and yellow. By using the inks together, the printer can create most colours of the rainbow. The reservoirs for these three inks and the print head are combined in the inkjet cartridge.

Most inkjet printers have a second cartridge containing a reservoir of black ink for high-quality text printing. A few low-cost printers have only one cartridge and mix the cyan, magenta and yellow inks to make black, but print quality for text documents is generally poor with such printers.

Some photo-oriented inkjets use special cartridges to create more realistic images. These may use up to six ink colours to produce a fuller range of tones. Only buy

Most inkjet printers give printouts in full colour, as well as black and white.

PC TIPS

When buying a printer – and especially a colour inkjet – ask to see samples of the printouts it can produce on plain paper. Beware of choosing a printer on the basis of its print quality on expensive coated paper only. If you are buying a printer for the first time, remember to get a printer cable. A manufacturer might not include it, and it is essential.

this type of printer if you're sure that you want top-quality photographs, as the extra complexity can add significantly to the price compared to a normal inkjet printer.

● Inkjet watchpoints

The inkjet cartridges must be replaced when the ink runs out, and they can be expensive to buy because many include part of the printer's electronics. Ink refill kits cut the cost.

Laser printers will give the professional quality you need for most black-and-white documents and images.

Inkjet printers can also be fussy about the paper they need. While ordinary copier paper is acceptable for text and simple illustrations, the best photo-quality printouts call for specially coated paper, which can be quite expensive. The coating is designed to produce clean, full colours with little or no paper wrinkling. Photographs printed on plain copier paper often look dull and have little contrast. It is important not to be too ambitious with home colour

inkjets. Low printing speeds and the high page costs of coated paper make it impractical to run off large quantities of colour prints on an inkjet printer. Just six copies of an A4 full-colour print will cost between £3 and £6 to produce and take anything from five to 15 minutes to print. The other disadvantage of colour inkjet printing is the fragility of the print. It can smear, especially when damp.

● Laser printers

If you don't need colour, but want the very best black-and-white print quality, there is only one choice: the laser printer. These print out high-quality documents quickly and you can print onto a wide range of paper sizes, labels and other formats. The printouts from a laser printer are also more robust than those from an inkjet; they are actually waterproof.

Personal laser printers for the home work in exactly the same way as their professional cousins. A laser beam scans across an electrically

Despite the high initial purchase price, laser printers can be economical to run if they are used sensibly.

charged cylinder (called a drum) leaving a pattern of dots to which toner (ink) particles stick. Once transferred on to the paper, heat melts the toner in place.

Laser printers can print several thousand sheets before the toner runs out. When it does, you simply buy a new cartridge. On most laser printers, the cartridge includes the drum, and replacements can be quite expensive. A few laser printers use separate drum and toner cartridges. These can be cheaper to run, as you rarely need to change the drum and the toner cartridge is cheaper.

Perfect printing

For most home computer users, a colour inkjet printer is the ideal choice – they are simple to use, versatile and, if you follow a few basic tips, reasonably inexpensive to run. We will show you how to get more from your printer.

Your printer will give you great results even if all you do is click the print button and never delve deeper into its capabilities. However, to really get the most out of your printer – the very best print quality and the optimum use of paper and ink – a little experimentation goes a long way.

● Before you buy

All you need to set up your home print shop are a printer, a cable to connect it to your PC and paper to use in your printer. If you haven't selected a printer yet, consider what you will use it for to guide you to the one best suited to your needs.

There are almost as many different uses of a printer as there are printers on sale – it's up to you to decide what you want to do: write letters, make greetings cards, print photographs or design menus, for example.

If you expect to be producing a lot of printed sheets, then the cost per page and printing speed are both important points to consider. Be wary of those less expensive printers that have only one cartridge instead of the more usual combination of one black ink and one colour ink cartridge (see pages 102–103). These can turn

out to be a false economy, as they must create black by blending colours, a process that can be wasteful. Look for a computer store that will print test pages for the various printers. You'll then have some samples to help you decide.

The ideal family printer comes bundled with software aimed at capturing children's attention and helping them to get the most out of the printer's many settings.

Some inkjet printers come with great family oriented software. Shop around and you'll find printers that can print transfers for your own T-shirt designs and models that can print on continuous paper so you can make long banners. Some printers come with software aimed specifically at children. A good example is Disney's Print Studio series which uses characters from *101 Dalmations*, *Toy Story* and other well known Disney classics to help guide children thorugh the trickier aspects of using a printer's features.

● Photographic quality

For more general A4 paper printing, most inkjet printers are capable of turning out impressive, almost photographic, quality images. This opens possibilities for all sorts of

The quality and detail that can be achieved with today's inkjet printers are stunning. Here's an almost photographic quality print-out from a Hewlett-Packard inkjet printer. The picture on the left is shown at actual size. On the right, we've zoomed right in to show the details of the dots that make up the image.

family albums and birthday cards. When you print photographs you'll find that the quality of paper makes a big difference to the final result.

● Hidden costs

A colour inkjet may be cheap to buy, but there are hidden costs behind the sales talk. The claims of hundreds of sheets of printing from a single colour cartridge must be listened to with caution. If you try to print full-page, full-colour pictures, you'll find that the ink runs out long before the number of printed pages quoted. Such figures are usually based on just 15 per cent colour ink on a page. This is reasonable for text pages with

small colour graphics, but if you intend to print full-page A4 designs, expect the life of your colour cartridge to be somewhat shorter.

● Printing on colour

If you want to produce pages with a solid colour background, then visit a local office supplier and ask about stocks of coloured paper. You'll find plain paper in various colours, as well as blank certificates, sheets of labels, business cards and colour designs. With a few lines of printing from your inkjet, these pages could look just as good as if you had printed the whole thing on plain white paper.

With imagination, you should be able to turn these blanks into party invitations, birthday and Christmas cards, club membership cards or menus. Using these ready-made blanks, you win several times over: you save money on ink, you save on design time and you also save print time because you're only printing your own colour graphics, not the whole page.

● Software control

The printer software is the key to getting the most from your printer. This is the software that lets your other programs control the printer. With the software, you can alter paper size and type and select the print quality you need. For the best results you can opt for fast, but less good quality, draft mode, or slower presentation mode.

Printouts from inkjets like this Hewlett-Packard DeskJet 845C look stunning, but make sure you keep paper and ink costs under control.

To access special features on your printer, click on Properties in the Print dialog box, which appears when you select the Print command. This opens a printer control page where your printer's options are displayed. Here you have a variety of paper types to select from, to match your print job.

SITES TO @ VISIT

You can use the Internet to download the latest software for your printer. This software is often revised to fix any bugs and to improve the printer's performance. Here are the Web sites of some of the leading printer manufacturers.

Epson:
www.epson.com/
Hewlett-Packard:
www.hp.com/
Canon:
www.canon.co.uk

Experimenting with your printer

Colour printers are great fun, but to make sure you don't waste time, ink and paper, you'll need to take the guesswork out of printing. Here's how to create your own reference pages to show what your printer can do.

GETTING THE best results out of your printer is a lot easier when you have a good idea of the full range of results this piece of hardware can actually deliver. For example, what types of print jobs benefit from special paper? Is plain copier paper suitable for printing children's paintings? Which typefaces will look best for the club newsletter?

By spending a little time creating some test pages, you'll have a ready reference to help you answer these questions. The following exercises will teach you more about your printer and help take the guesswork out of colour printing.

● Test different types of paper

You can use Word to create sample pages that are representative of the types of documents you print. If you use colourful WordArt, clip art and/or your own graphics (see pages 46–49), be sure to add them to your samples. Try to fit them on to one page to save paper.

Now print this page on a selection of different paper types (your printer manual will tell you which types of paper your printer can use). You'll need to buy some pages of each type to do this, but the investment is well worth it. Look closely at the print quality for each type of object on

You can create a font reference document to show all the fonts on your PC. You'll be able to see more detail in the printed letters than you can on your computer screen.

your page. Try to get a feel for which type of paper is worth the extra investment and which is not.

Clearly name each paper type and store these printed pages in a file by your printer, so that whenever you need to print something out of the ordinary, you can simply pull out the file and find the best paper to use.

● Compile a font list

It's important to make sure that you choose the right font (or typeface) for a job. Here's how to print your own font guide: open Word and type in the names of the fonts listed in the font box, one font to a line. Now select each line in turn, and change the font to correspond with its name (see pages 36–37).

Again, print out the page and store it in your printed samples file. When you need to create something special, you can make sense of all those font names at a glance. You'll find that it's a lot easier to select fonts from your printed page than it is from the computer screen.

● Create a colour swatch

The biggest area of guesswork comes when you print colours. Computer screens and inkjet printer colours rarely match perfectly because they work in very different ways.

To remove the guesswork, print a colour swatch page. You can use this like the paint booklets you get from DIY stores. With a single page of colour squares to choose from, you can choose colours with confidence.

Many Windows programs have a basic palette of around 40 colours. You can use Excel to create a grid of squares with a different colour in each (see pages 58–59). This will provide a simple guide; print it on the different types of paper to see how the paper quality affects the colour. Add these pages to your printer reference file.

If you haven't got Excel, use Paint. You can draw rectangles in colours from the palette at the bottom of the Paint window (see pages 64–65).

Try using Excel to make a simple colour swatch page – just colour each cell. Copy the layout of the drop-down colour palette so you know which colour is which.

Adding a printer to your PC

Don't be put off by the task of adding a printer to your system. With this guide and the helpfulness of Windows, you'll quickly be up and running.

ONCE YOU'VE bought your printer, you're only a few steps away from printing your first pages.

● Unpacking
First, remove the printer and its accessories from its packing material. Keep the cardboard shapes and sticky tape used to hold the printer parts in position while in transit.

● Finding space
Now find a space that's close enough to connect the printer to your PC and also accessible enough for adding and removing paper.

● Insert paper and cartridge(s)
Place some paper in the printer. Then connect the printer power supply and follow the printer manual's instructions for inserting the inkjet or laser printer cartridges. For the moment, keep your computer switched off.

● Connect the printer to the PC
The physical connections are easy to follow. Check our guide (Connecting the printer and computer, below) to see exactly what goes where.

● Switch on
First turn the printer on, then your computer. This ensures that Windows can try to automatically detect the new printer. A message will appear on your computer screen, asking for the software for the printer. Insert the CD provided with the printer when it is requested.

If Windows doesn't spot your new printer, the printer manual will show you how to install the software.

● Print test page
When all the steps have been carried out, Windows will ask you if you want to print out a test page. Click on the OK button, and your printer will now start working.

● Set default printer
Click the Yes button when Windows asks you if you want the printer to be the default printer. This ensures that your printed pages go direct to this printer without requiring further intervention from you.

● Restart the computer
Restart Windows, and you'll be able to use your new printer right away.

Once you have selected the printer, its icon appears in the Printers and Faxes folder. The tick indicates that it has been selected as the default printer.

Connecting the printer and computer

Connecting a printer to your computer is easy: there's only one lead and it only fits one way round, so you needn't worry about making any mistakes. Here's your guide to trouble-free printer connection.

Most printers use a USB cable (as illustrated right) to connect to a computer but older printers use a parallel cable – check the printer manual for information on the right procedure. **For USB connections**, you do not need to switch off the computer. Plug the printer power cable into the wall socket and the power socket into the printer. Connect the computer and printer using the printer cable. With a USB printer cable, the small square plug fits into the socket on the back of the printer. The other end of the USB cable will have a slim, rectangular plug to fit the computer; your PC will probably have 2 or more USB sockets – use any one.
For parallel connections, make sure that your computer is switched off before you start. With a parallel printer cable, the larger plug fits into the socket at the back of the printer. Two clips hold the plug securely. The other end of the parallel printer cable fits into a socket on the back of the computer, often labelled LPT1. Use the plug's two screws to hold it in place. Switch on the printer first, then the computer.

❶ All computers have 2 or 3 USB sockets at the back; many also have some sockets on the front or even on the keyboard or screen. For a printer, one at the back is normally most convenient. A parallel socket is always at the back of the printer: it's fairly easy to spot because PCs only have one socket of this type.

❷ The printer cable should be long enough to give some choice of printer placement, but not so long that it gets snarled up with others.

❸ This printer uses an external mains adaptor. Other printers will use a standard mains lead for their power supply.

❹ The other end of the printer cable fits into the printer. The long socket with clips below the USB socket is for a parallel connection.

Home Learning & Leisure

Choosing your software

Selecting home learning software is a tricky business because there are so many titles on the market. So what should you look for when you go out to buy your educational programs?

Your PC is superb for home learning, but however impressive your hardware, it's useless without good software. There are three basic types of home learning software: reference, study and 'edutainment'.

CD-ROMs and DVDs store vast amounts of information, so reference software, such as Microsoft's *Encarta Reference Library 2002* (see pages 112–113) and Dorling Kindersley's *Millennium 20th Century Day by Day*, usually come in this format.

Whereas books deliver text and pictures only, software resources like these provide a multimedia experience, with extras like sound, video and interactive features. However, it's important that you are able to find your way to the facts you want without too much trouble, so look for a title with a powerful but simple-to-use search engine.

Value for money is important when assessing software. Programs aren't cheap, so look for depth of content and different levels of complexity.

OUT THERE

A wide selection of home learning software is available from computer superstores and other specialist outfits. Most companies will also supply software direct via mail order – if you find one type of program is particularly suited to your family's needs, why not contact the publisher to get a catalogue of its other titles?

The majority of software makers have Web sites enabling you to download demonstration versions and buy the software online. You can also check the system requirements to make sure that your chosen software is XP compatible.

The hallmark of good educational software is an ability to make the learning experience enjoyable, not only for the student, but for the whole family. Look for software which uses all the advantages of Multimedia and interactivity that the home computer can bring.

● **Study software**
Study software is designed to help you in developing a specific skill or learning a subject. Examples include the DK *Test for Success* series (see pages 118–119) and *Guide to Better Photography* or *Driving Test Success 2001/2002* from the extensive range offered by Focus Multimedia.

This type of software usually relies on a degree of repetition, but the key is whether the exercises are fun. Look out for programs that give feedback to the user via test results and advice on areas where further practice is needed.

Join Little Polar Bear and his friends on this charming Arctic adventure of the same name, and participate in a series of games and challenges along the way.

Help Rainbow Fish find his stolen scales by completing a range of activities, including logic puzzles and recognizing melodies, in the Rainbow Fish CD-ROM.

● Edutainment software

The aim of edutainment software is to entertain as well as educate. Foremost in this category is DK's CD-ROM range which includes challenging educational games with colourful graphics such as *Little Polar Bear* and *Rainbow Fish* for three- to seven-year-olds (see pages 122–125).

When choosing this type of program look for a balance between learning and enjoyment. These titles encourage children to use a wide range of skills such as reading, counting, telling the time, thinking creatively, problem-solving, linking words and pictures, and developing mouse and cursor skills.

Most software boasts that it is interactive, but real interactivity is much more than just clicking on-screen buttons. Programs should encourage children to get involved in the content by giving them

Software can be expensive, so put plenty of thought into the type you want and consider whether it is suitable for your intended uses and the type of computer you have.

an opportunity to use their own creative abilities, or by providing follow-up activities.

Uncle Albert's Magical Album, again from the DK range, is packed with amazing stories, photographs, experiments and hidden treasure. Seven- to twelve-year-olds will have many hours of fun as they join an interactive treasure quest by using all the tools, objects and animals inside the album to unlock secret pages.

● Looking good

Any software, whether for children or adults, has to be visually stimulating. It's important to check the quality of

the graphics (they may be enhanced on the packaging so what you see isn't necessarily what you get). If children find software boring, they won't use it. When you buy a book you can flip through it to see if it's suitable, but software comes in shrink-wrapped boxes so you can't examine it. However, it's worth asking for an in-store demonstration or, better still ask friends to show you packages which their children enjoyed so you can try before you buy.

SOFTWARE CHECKLIST

Will the program run on your computer?

Is the target age range appropriate?

Will the software do what you want it to?

Is it easy to use?

Is it bright, attractive and interactive?

Are support materials included in the package?

Does it represent good value for money?

Can you try before you buy?

Facts at your fingertips

A single CD-ROM encyclopedia can store all the information you would expect to find in a multi-volume printed set – with the added bonus of sound, videos and animation.

When was the last time you looked at a printed encyclopedia, reading articles and studying the pictures and tables? If you can't remember, you're like most other people. After an initial flurry of use, encyclopedias are usually placed on a bookshelf and left to gather dust.

Part of the reason for this is that encyclopedias contain huge amounts of information. They're perfect when you want to look up something specific, but if you want to read more about a topic, you can spend a lot of time wading through the index, flicking through pages and cross-referencing other volumes in the series. Often, more time is spent looking for information than digesting it.

● CD-ROMs to the rescue

Enter the CD-ROM – a disc similar to the audio CDs you buy in music stores. Instead of just storing music, however, the CD-ROM contains text, pictures, graphics and sound that can all be accessed on your PC. CD-ROMs – and their even more capacious cousin, the DVD – make ideal storage systems for encyclopedias because they can hold vast amounts of information. They are good value for money and can be used again and again, whenever your child has a new homework topic, or when you need to look something up yourself. What's more, because they are interactive, CD-ROMs make learning an enjoyable experience for children.

Traditional leatherbound encyclopedias face strong competition from one of the most exciting developments in home learning – the CD-ROM encyclopedia. These discs contain huge amounts of visual and written information that can be explored at the click of the mouse button. They also make searching for information easy.

WHAT HARDWARE?

Most CD-ROM or DVD-ROM programs specify a minimum requirement for PC hardware. Before buying any program, look at the packaging and find the system requirements panel; this lists the hardware and software needed. Although any PC that's already running Windows XP is likely to meet the hardware requirements of most Multimedia programs, you must remember to check. For example, some fast-paced 3D action games require specific types of 3D graphics card.

● An encyclopedia for the family

Microsoft's *Encarta Encyclopedia Deluxe 2002* is the latest version of one of the best-known CD-ROM encyclopedias. It has thousands of articles, covering topics from arts, sport, history and religion, through to current events, with cross-referencing to make searching easy. It also features videos, sound clips, music clips, map locations and Web links.

When you start *Encarta*, the Home screen displays a Pinpointer window which shows a complete alphabetical list of all articles on the database. Alternatively, just type a word or phrase into the Find box and click on GO. A full list of matches is then displayed – just click on an entry to go to that page.

The Multimedia sections are great fun, especially the 3D virtual tours in which the user can walk around ancient locations such as the Colosseum or look at the inside of the Space Shuttle.

Encarta is suitable for secondary school pupils and college students, as well as fact-hungry adults. Young children will love seeing a spider spin its web or taking part in one of the interactive learning games.

If you are looking for the ultimate reference source, the *Encarta Reference Library 2002* combines three titles: the *Encarta Encyclopedia Deluxe*, *Dictionary and Thesaurus* and the *Interactive World Atlas*.

Encarta (above) uses pictures, text and animation to make the learning experience more enjoyable. The pages are packed with links so that you can easily 'read around' a topic.

The colourful screen of Encyclopedia Britannica Deluxe 2002 (left) lets you explore articles, timelines, an atlas and a wide range of topics related to the National Curriculum.

INFORMATION SEARCH

With a little bit of practice, you will soon learn how to find what you want easily and quickly. These reference CD-ROMs have simple search interfaces, where you key in a topic and let your computer do the hard work of searching through data. However, if you can't find what you're looking for immediately, don't give up. Double-click on the main entry and you will bring up a list of sub-topics. Often you will find multimedia elements such as sound clips, photographs and video sequences. Most encyclopedias also have links to relevant Web sites.

CONTACT POINTS

Hutchinson Encyclopedia 2002
Price: £19.99*
Focus Multimedia
Tel: 0500 053 725 or 01889 579 977
www.focusmm.co.uk

Encarta Encyclopedia Deluxe 2002
Price: £21.99*
Encarta Reference Library 2002
Price: £29.99*
Microsoft
Tel: 0345 002 000
www.microsoft.com/uk

Encyclopedia Britannica Deluxe 2002
Price: from £29.99*
Encyclopedia Britannica Inc
Tel: 0808 100 7100
www.britannica.com   *UK prices

● Knowledge in depth

Sometimes CD-based encyclopedias can appear a bit lightweight. They might be full of pictures and video clips, but if you want to investigate a particular interest in depth, they can be disappointing. If you're looking for something with more pedigree and heavyweight coverage, try *Encyclopedia Britannica Deluxe 2002*, the CD-ROM version of the *Encyclopedia Britannica*, a respected source of knowledge since 1768.

The *Encyclopedia Britannica Deluxe 2002* is a truly vast resource, containing more than 85,000 articles and 12,000 photographs, 360-degree panoramas, animations and video clips. Like the *Encarta Reference Library 2002*, it also includes a dictionary and world atlas.

Those familiar with the Internet will notice that *Britannica*'s opening screen is very similar to a Web site. Don't be put off by this if you know nothing about the Web because *Britannica* is very user-friendly. Three main ways of accessing this treasure house of information are offered: Search, A-Z Britannica or Knowledge Navigator. These allow you to type in a topic, ask a question or explore a visual index of subjects. Whether you are a researcher, quiz fan, student or simply enjoy reading and learning, you will find this software invaluable.

Increase your word power

When preparing a document, a CD-ROM dictionary not only helps you check the spelling and origin of a word – it can also give you instant access to a wealth of detailed reference material.

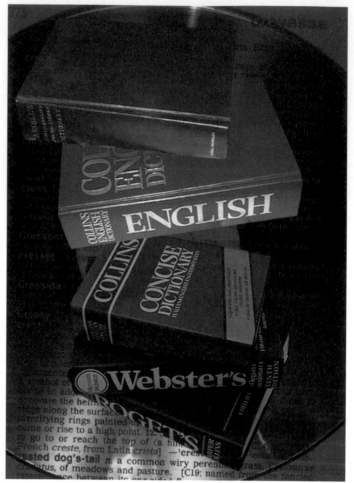

Few books that we use frequently are as useful as a dictionary – and few are as bulky. The more detailed they are, the heavier they are, and the longer you might have to spend looking for what you're after. But it doesn't have to be like that; with a software dictionary or other reference work, all your information fits on one CD-ROM. Browsing and searching is thus faster and more convenient.

You might be used to running the spelling checker over any documents you write in Word and you might even have tried Word's thesaurus function to search for new or different words to use (we will cover these Word functions later in the course). But, while these functions are fine for ensuring the accuracy of documents, reference CD-ROMs do much more. Not only will they help your spelling, they can also tell you the definition and origins of a word and lead you to quotes, facts and other information to inspire and inform you. With a good reference CD-ROM at your fingertips, you will never be at a loss for words again.

● **Much more than words**

The *Encarta Reference Library 2002* is one such comprehensive collection of reference resources.

In addition to the encyclopedia (see page 113), it includes a combined dictionary and thesaurus. The dictionary facility can be used quite independently to check on correct spellings or to find the definition or origin of a word. The thesaurus will automatically give you a list of synonyms and, where appropriate, antonyms for the chosen word.

The combined dictionary and thesaurus in Microsoft's Encarta Reference Library 2002 is intrinsically linked to the other features in the package. For example, if you come across the word 'democracy' and want to check on its origins, a simple click of the mouse takes you to the dictionary.

Although the actual content of the dictionary may not be as extensive as that found in a stand-alone version, where the *Encarta Reference Library 2002* undoubtedly scores is in the links it supplies to the other features of the software. By simply clicking on a word in an article, the dictionary screen will instantly appear, giving you further information.

The Researcher facility allows you to collect and organize text and pictures from *Encarta* and the Web facility to create your own reports and projects. Every time you use the software you have the option to update the content with the latest articles and Web links. Through the *Encarta* online Web site it also gives you access to a wealth of additional learning areas such as a useful multilingual dictionary.

Encarta makes the information more accessible by presenting it in an exciting way. With its dynamic use of sound, video and animation, this is a true Multimedia resource that should appeal to a wide range of age groups.

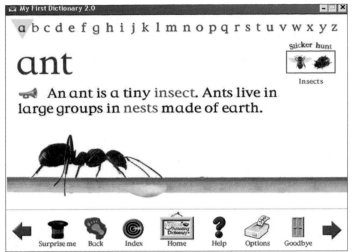

With DK's My First Dictionary *learning to spell becomes a fun-filled activity which will capture the imagination of children aged three to seven.*

One of the range of brightly illustrated activities is the Spell it section, where you can choose from three different levels according to age and ability.

● A basic dictionary

Not everyone wants a multi-volume reference work, however. If you are just looking for a dictionary that you can dip into at the click of a mouse, the *Concise Oxford Dictionary (10th Edition)* is available as a stand-alone reference work boasting entries for over 240,000 words, phrases and definitions. Clear, simple screens make searching for words an easy and straightforward procedure.

● Kids' reference

The reference works mentioned so far are aimed at the adult user. Children, however, are not neglected and of

The Concise Oxford Dictionary *CD-ROM does the thumbing of pages for you, quickly finding the word you're looking for.*

particular note is a CD-ROM from Dorling Kindersley which covers ages three to seven.

My First Dictionary comes in a package filled with a range of activity material for children. The CD-ROM itself is a bright and breezy lexicon of over 1,000 words, all illustrated and supported by spoken sound recordings.

The CD-ROM works in a simple enough way for young children to master without much parental intervention. There are several rewarding word games to test what children have learned while they've been using the software and every dictionary screen visited gives the user a gold reward star – always popular with this age group.

In the spelling section, there are three different levels to work through in order that the child can learn how to spell 180 words.

The CD-ROM is designed to work sympathetically with the higher end of the age group, so the spoken explanations and animations can be turned off for these older children.

The printed part of the package includes educational games with animal stickers to match up to words as well as a fun treasure hunt. There are also guidelines for parents on how to use the disc with children.

SITES TO @ VISIT

Yahoo!
www.yahoo.co.uk
Yahoo! has divided its reference sites into different subject areas, such as Computing, Language and Science, so choose the one you think is the best match.

Dorling Kindersley
www.gsp.cc
Dorling Kindersley's Multimedia range is now published by GSP. Visit the GSP site to find out more about the extensive range of educational Dorling Kindersley CD-ROMs.

Microsoft
www.microsoft.com/uk
Use the search facility on this site to discover more information about Microsoft's *Encarta* range.

CONTACT POINTS

Encarta Reference Library 2002
Price: £29.99*
Microsoft
Tel: 0345 002 000
www.microsoft.com/uk

Concise Oxford Dictionary (10th Edition)
Price: £19.99*
Oxford University Press
Tel: 01536 741 727
www.oup.co.uk

DK My First Dictionary
Price: £19.99*
GSP
Tel: 01480 496 666
www.gsp.cc

*UK prices

Maths made easy

Mastering the mysteries of maths can be made a little easier if you employ the services of your own desk-based teacher – and you may even find yourself enjoying it!

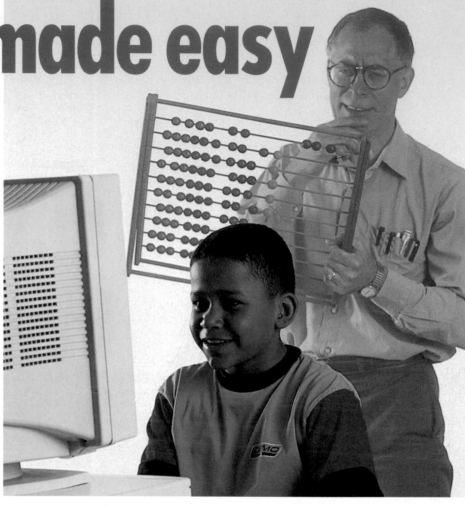

Maths seems to be one of those subjects at which you are either naturally good or you need help. If you fall into the latter category – or you are trying to teach somebody who does – you'll find that your computer can help in ways that you may never have imagined.

● Making maths easier

There are many ways in which you can use your computer to make maths easier. You can perform simple calculations using the calculator that comes as part of Windows (see pages 12–13). You can also use an Excel spreadsheet to help with the domestic finances (see pages 54–55). There are even personal finance packages, such as the Microsoft *Money 2002* series and Intuit's *Quicken 2002*, which specialize in helping you keep track of your finances.

When it comes to the basics of learning and mastering maths, you'll also find programs to help and inspire

you, no matter what age you are or what stage you may be at with your maths lessons.

● Covering all age groups

These educational programs go all the way from the fun through to the serious. They also cover all ages, from pre-school to GCSE level and beyond. In the fun category, there are titles such as *Zoombinis Mountain Rescue* from Mindscape.

Modern PC-based programs are far removed from the traditional methods of teaching mathematics. Some of them are so much fun that the essential key to success with numbers – practice – isn't a problem.

Zoombinis Mountain Rescue combines simple maths with logic skills. It's all wrapped up in a highly enjoyable game environment that will delight adults as much as the young children for whom it is intended.

Zoombinis are a cute race of little creatures with many different characteristics. Some have red noses, others purple, some green; some have feet, others have skates and some have springs. A group of them are trapped on a mysterious mountain and you must recruit a team of 16 Zoombinis for a rescue mission. The team is picked according to their features (noses, hair, eyes, feet) and only two must be identical.

The creatures set off from their home town of Zoombiniville and, to help them, you must successfuly explore dangerous and puzzle-packed

The Learning Company's Zoombinis Mountain Rescue uses a cartoon atmosphere instead of the more conventional illustrations found in most maths books.

In this software, maths is a means to an end – saving the Zoombinis from disaster. This is the magic ingredient that captures youngsters' imaginations.

mountain passages such as Beetle Bug Alley and Turtle Hurdle. Each perilous puzzle you solve leads to another more difficult challenge.

The basic concept of the program is to teach maths without the use of numbers but through a series of entertaining games. For example, Boolie Boggle is an engrossing pinball game which actually teaches binary addition. Other skills such as algebraic thinking and data sorting are all taught by means of these little creatures and 3D mazes rather than formulas and numbers.

There are three levels of difficulty and the games are accompanied by lively music and narration.

● Serious stuff

On the more serious level, one of the most effective maths software titles is *StudyWorks* from Mathsoft, which is appropriate for serious maths students. It has easy-to-understand instructions and examples, and all the formulae are laid out on screen.

For help with GCSE preparation, programs such as Europress' *GCSE Maths* are designed to cover the complete curriculum for all examining boards. There are 190 separate subjects split into four maths areas: Number; Algebra; Shape, Space and measurement; and Handling data.

The topics are covered in step-by-step exercises and five historical maths mentors – from Pythagorus to Charles Babbage – are on hand to guide pupils through them. *GCSE Maths* also has an exam mode that poses sets of 16 questions in each of the four maths areas; the student is allowed 45 minutes to answer them. Each time the exam mode is run, a different exam is presented, so passing isn't just a matter of learning the right answers by rote.

There are many Internet sites to help you with maths. One such is Freeserve's learning site.

BREAKAWAY MATHS

Breakaway Maths is aimed at pupils aged between seven and 12 who are experiencing difficulty with maths.

In this program, maths problems are set within the context of the Breakaway Theme Park, which is based on the Alton Towers theme park in Staffordshire, England. As the pupil moves around the theme park – accompanied by Rupa, Lisa, Nicky and David – he or she has to solve activity or investigation problems.

Activity problems consist of two groups of up to 10 questions. These are set at the beginning of a ride. To experience the ride – such as the terrifying Nemesis – you must first answer 10 questions. Halfway through you have to answer the next 10 questions in order to finish the ride. Investigation problems are set at attractions around the theme park, such

Some maths software, such as Breakaway Maths, can harness the thrills and spills of popular adventures to help motivate children to learn.

The BBC's Bitesize Revision pages provide an excellent online resource for GCSE students. This maths page, for example, shows some simple questions to start off with.

Whatever your maths needs, from simple concepts to complex problems, there's software to help you.

● Internet help

There are also considerable resources on the Internet. In fact, the Internet has become a great place for learning, especially when it comes to that crucial exam revision time. There are several sites that give solid help in maths (and many other subjects). One of the best examples is the BBC's GCSE revision section (www.bbc.co.uk/schools/gcsebitesize/maths). Key topics are covered and

as the souvenir shop, restaurant and so on. All the questions are pitched at the appropriate level, which is set according to an assessment exercise done when the child first starts *Breakaway Maths*.

each subsection is accompanied by its own test. The Counton Web site (www.counton.org) offers help with maths for all ages from virtual games to GCSE and A-level attainment tests. Freescrve's Learning channel (http://www.freeserve.com/learning) gives key revision points and tests in all the topic areas from Key Stage 3 through to A-level maths.

Successful maths exams

It's often difficult for parents to help children with school work, but now your computer can run programs that guide them all the way – from SATs to GCSEs.

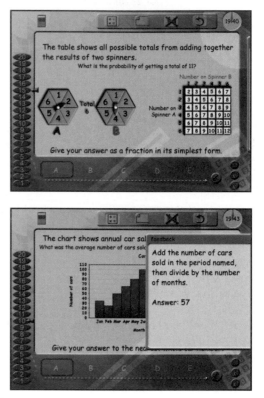

The SATs Tests CD-ROMs from Europress are all about making progress in the subject being studied – in this case maths – and preparing the student for the exam, with clear graphics to aid comprehension.

Almost as soon as children start school these days, they are required to begin sitting exams. Although these don't all involve the child sitting formally in an examining hall, the results are taken seriously by schools.

These early tests, for children as young as seven, are known as Standard Assessment Tests (SATs). Schools keen to work their way up the annual league tables – published in national newspapers – aim for good results in these tests.

● Practice makes perfect
In reality, the SATs exams for seven-year-olds are low-key, so children should not be troubled by exam nerves. But often parents – and even

teachers – who are aware of looming SATs exams, pass down any anxiety they have to the children who have to sit them. With a little experience and preparation, even seven-year-olds will

Some Multimedia software hides its educational content in games and stories. That's fine for younger children, but SATs Tests from Europress is focused on passing exams.

be able to give a true account of their abilities, unaffected by the pressure of the exam environment. But parents are not always the best people to help, especially in subjects perhaps long-forgotten, such as science and, of course, the much-feared maths.

● The equation for success
Even if you haven't forgotten all your own school work, your help could be counter-productive unless you are clued-up on exactly what the current National Curriculum includes. That's where programs like the *SATs Tests*

It's possible to identify how well the student is doing by reviewing previously taken SATs tests (above). Sets of questions can be tailor-made (below) to include only weaker areas, but should also include strong categories so the student doesn't become too discouraged.

series of CD-ROMs from Europress come in. The CDs cover maths for 7, 11 and 14 year olds. These are not Multimedia products with the educational content of the program hidden behind a colourful facade but sets of realistic questions presented in such a way as to make the actual exam, when the time comes, seem more familiar and less daunting. This means that the student's results are less likely to be distorted by test nerves.

● Parental guidance

The *SATs tests* program for 11-year-olds is designed for children to use either with or without their parents'

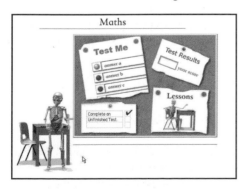

Seemore Skinless, the brainy skeleton, plays the madcap host for Dorling Kindersley's Test for Success – Maths.

help. The program can be used in various ways, such as questions with immediate feedback or in test mode, working against the clock. It contains over 4,000 questions, including a National Curriculum Level 6 section. A comprehensive results section helps students, parents and teachers assess the progress of the user. Tests can be structured to concentrate on any or all of the 20 topics.

● Test yourself

In the *Test for Success* series of education CD-ROMs, Dorling Kindersley has combined the much-loved bright and colourful design of its books with interactive Multimedia to help introduce key concepts. The *Test for Success Age 11* versions of the CD-ROMs are aimed at children aged between seven and 11, helping them to gain the vital skills they need during their crucial primary years. *Test for Success – Maths* is written by primary school teachers and supports the National Curriculum Key Stage 2.

To capture young children's attention, a zany skeleton, Seemore Skinless, accompanies them through the lessons. For each topic, he jokes and fools a little, while helping the teacher/narrator introduce and explain the basic maths concepts. Both the narrator and Seemore praise correct answers.

Children start by entering their name and age, and the software generates an appropriate set of lessons. During each lesson there are several on-screen questions to assess how much the child has learned. The questions are graded to cover the youngest to oldest child as well as to test for some advanced abilities. Several children can use the program and it stores their results separately.

Test for Success Age 14 Maths is a valuable learning tool for Key Stage 3. There are over 1,300 interactive questions with full explanations so they teach as they test. A useful key points section can be printed out for use in revision. Progress records help to identify weaknesses and target areas for further study.

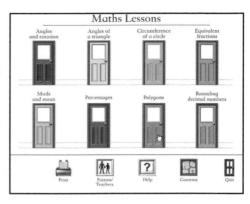

Once the child has entered their name and age, the Test for Success – Maths program assesses their level and generates an appropriate set of maths concepts.

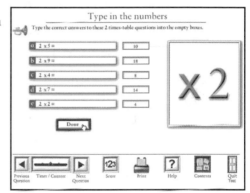

All of the screens in Test for Success – Maths use the same clear design philosophy of Dorling Kindersley's books.

Test for Success – Maths has a password-protected area that lets parents or teachers see how well each child is progressing.

The world on a disc

With a CD-ROM atlas you can experience sights and sounds from anywhere in the world – without even leaving the comfort of your own home.

Microsoft's Encarta Interactive World Atlas *is more than just a reference guide to the countries of the world: it also explains the facts behind the Earth's makeup.*

Select a Map Trek and audio and visual clips help to give you a better insight into the diverse nature of the planet and the different peoples of the world.

Incredible 3D virtual flights allow you to look at the world in which we live from every conceivable angle – from city maps at street level, to this view from space.

There are few books as interesting or as instructive as a good atlas, with its combination of detailed maps, fascinating statistics and explanations of how the Earth has developed since its origins. But can the CD-ROM atlas outdo its printed counterpart in terms of presentation and detail?

In many respects it can, through the addition of elements, such as video, photographs and sound, together with the use of dynamic links between different types of information. In a printed atlas, you would have to look at a map page, find the relevant statistical page,

then turn to yet another section to find out about the physical geography of the area you are considering. Yet, with a CD-ROM atlas, a few clicks of the mouse will bring up all that data on your screen as the questions present themselves – and also throw in a video clip with narration or music for good measure. As a result, you can learn the broadest aspects of geography in a way that often feels more natural than using a book.

● **The world at your fingertips**
The *Interactive World Atlas* which is incorporated in the *Microsoft Encarta Reference Library 2002* demonstrates this well.

The core information itself is first class and the maps are clear and attractive, letting you zoom in close to see a greater amount of detail or zoom out to satellite views to get the bigger picture. Country articles give

Dorling Kindersley's Become A World Explorer *is far more than just an atlas on CD-ROM. Featuring dazzling animations, 3D effects and interactive games, this activity pack will take your child on a fun-packed learning adventure.*

you not only the geography but also the history, language and customs, accompanied by a rich variety of photographs. Nearly everywhere on the globe has an associated sound clip featuring typical music of the region.

If you are planning an exotic holiday you can learn useful phrases in scores of languages from Albanian to Zulu. You can even take a virtual holiday – instead of simply looking at a map or photographs of your chosen destination, you can hear the national anthem and listen to the language via a live radio broadcast.

A few clicks of the mouse will take you through 360-degree panoramic views of natural wonders such as Mount Everest and famous landmarks such as Alcatraz, with the bonus of historical and cultural tour notes.

● Globetrotters' guides

Dorling Kindersley's *Eyewitness World Atlas* is similarly strong on reference material, with the latest version featuring interactive maps and exciting 3D graphics. Presented as a hybrid atlas/encyclopedia/gazetteer, it is ideal for 11- to 16-year-olds and supports the school curriculum up to GCSE level.

The *WWF Interactive World Atlas* from Focus Multimedia lacks some of the finesse of the Microsoft and Dorling Kindersley atlases, but is still useful and informative. While the large-scale maps are not particularly attractive, they improve when you zoom in. You can then click on the signposts dotted around to get detailed local information, such as the area of a lake in Sweden.

CONTACT POINTS

Encarta Reference Library 2002
Price: £29.99*
Microsoft
Tel: 0345 002 000
www.microsoft.com/uk

DK Eyewitness World Atlas
DK Become a World Explorer
Price of each: £19.99*
GSP
Tel: 01480 496 666
www.gsp.cc

WWF Interactive World Atlas
Price: £9.99*
Focus Multimedia
Tel: 0500 053 725 or
01889 579 977
www.focusmm.co.uk

UK Prices*

Become A World Explorer, from Dorling Kindersley, is not exactly an atlas but rather a fun globetrotter's guide that will keep any six- to ten-year-old interested. It has easy-to-use search engines and over 600 pop-up fact boxes. Children can explore the world in a global treasure hunt, collect hundreds of virtual stickers, send postcards to their friends from any continent, and learn about different cultures from the 16 videos. There is also an educational quiz to test and reinforce your child's knowledge.

World wise

Dorling Kindersley's *Eyewitness World Atlas* is a comprehensive world guide.

Helping to put you in the picture

Remarkable 3D flythrough videos give you a breath-taking bird's-eye view of our planet and help to bring faraway places to life.

Find your way around the planet

Simple navigational tools allow you access to high quality interactive maps and background information on every nation in the world.

Know the global facts

Detailed charts and graphs provide an in-depth examination of every country. You can compare statistics between one nation and another and export data into your own applications.

Games for all

Are PC games all as violent and unsuitable for children as they are made out to be? The simple answer is 'No'. Choose your games carefully and they will provide education and entertainment for all the family.

It was not long ago that many people were transfixed by the sight of a simple white dot as they batted it from one side of the screen to the other. Today, however, this classic tennis game, called *Pong*, would keep the average game-player's attention for only a relatively short time.

Computer games have developed quickly from simple exercises to Multimedia experiences that seem to have more in common with television or the movies. Today's Multimedia PCs can have CD-quality stereo sound and a monitor that can display millions of colours to satisfy your ears and eyes, while the keys on the keyboard and the mouse will keep your hands busy. The program creator can put many different elements into a game, and there are thousands of games available.

● Choose carefully

Just as a video shop contains films that are suitable only for informed adults, the range of computer game titles includes many which are inappropriate for family use. Parents should use the same judgement on the suitability of a computer game as they would over a rented video. One of the best ways to do this is to check the game packaging for information about the age-group at which the game is aimed. Reading reviews of games also gives a good indication of whether they are actually suitable for the whole family to use.

You can also look for games which have parental control settings. These contain versions for adults and children. When the game is loaded, parents can set a secret password which prevents children from accessing the adult aspects of the game, but still allows children to enjoy a perfectly playable version.

● Check points

The number, range and content of games are extremely confusing. Many people select games on the

Games such as SimCity 3000, Age of Empires, Rollercoaster Tycoon and Star Trek are not only fun for all the family, but in their own way, can be an educational experience as well.

BEFORE YOU BUY

When buying a game, look on the box for the suitable age indicator that warns parents of the potential violence content of a game. This usually shows the age range that the game was designed for, such as 3–10, 7–11, 11–14 or 18+.

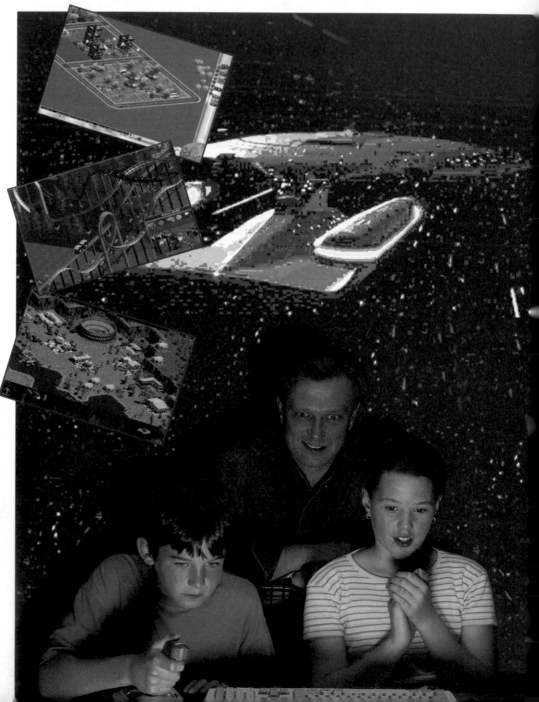

recommendation of friends or work colleagues, but what if you want to choose something new? The first point to consider is who the game is for. If it is solely for you, then you can choose a title that you find interesting personally. If it is for other members of your family too, you can choose a game with wider appeal.

Next, you need to be sure that the game will work on your computer. Look carefully at the minimum PC requirements printed on the packaging. Although most games are now released on CD-ROM, a small but increasing number of DVD games are coming out; these of course require a PC with a DVD-drive.

Another point to bear in mind is what the game is for. Many games are purely for the player's enjoyment. Others have a strong educational content – some specifically aimed at children to help them to practise the topics they are learning about at school, and some designed for adults who may want to explore a new area of learning. Some of the best family games successfully combine entertainment with education.

● Games to suit every taste

When you look at the range of games stacked on the shelves of high street shops and PC superstores, you soon realize that there is a title to suit most tastes and age groups. Choosing one to entertain you can be baffling, even if you have a general idea of the type of game you want.

One of the largest group of games is strategy, or mind, games (see pages

128–129). Mainly aimed at adults, these are games that you could easily find occupying a whole weekend. The best strategy games present you with a scenario in which you have to survive and thrive. A good example is *Civilization: Call To Power*, which casts you as the leader of a tribe. By making political, military, diplomatic, technological and economic decisions, your goal is to improve the fortunes and power of your people. Every decision you make has repercussions which you will have to live with in the future. The aim is to become the dominant people on Earth.

● An awfully big adventure

Adventure gaming is one of the oldest genres, dating back to the earliest mainframe computers. This type of game is played out in a large number of beautifully drawn locations. Depending on the plot, these can be anything from a bleak cityscape to a tongue-in-cheek Caribbean pirate island. Or, in the case of *Star Trek Bridge Commander*, you can take control of the Enterprise from Captain Picard's chair and explore the entire universe.

Unlike other game styles, lateral thinking is the prime requisite for adventure games. Controlling your

Lead your civilization to world supremacy by manipulating destiny from the Stone Age to the year AD 3000. Call To Power contains detailed information on a huge range of historical technologies, concepts and events.

on-screen character, you must travel from place to place, as the storyline and your quest within it demands, seeking clues and meeting various helpful, knowledgeable or unsavoury characters. Interacting with these characters plays an equal part with the manipulation of items in your inventory, as you use anything and everything in your possession to reach your goal.

The other prerequisite for the majority of adventure games is a sense of humour. Unlike many other games, humour plays a big part in most adventure titles and can be surprisingly subtle and clever. Some games run the full gamut of cinematic

Combine a good game with the Internet and you get a great game. With Monster Truck Madness 2, you log on to a special Internet site, choose your vehicle and race against players around the world – for the cost of a local phone call.

LONG PLAY?

There is a great debate about whether computer games are bad for children, and as with many arguments the answer lies somewhere between two opposing points of view. Of course, every case is different, but, generally, moderate game playing can be instructive, particularly if the game is educational. Children can learn from the content of the game, and, just from the act of playing, will even improve their keyboard and mouse skills. They might also learn more about how the computer works.

CHECKPOINT ✔

WILL IT WORK ON MY PC?

Check on the packaging to make sure the game is compatible with your computer. This information will usually be under the heading 'Minimum Requirements'. This gives details of the following requirements of a game:

- ☑ the type of computer processor (Pentium II, III or 4) and its speed (given in megahertz or 'MHz')
- ☑ minimum memory requirements (RAM)
- ☑ number of on-screen colours
- ☑ sound card
- ☑ operating system (make sure the game is guaranteed for Windows XP)
- ☑ 3D graphics accelerator
- ☑ the type of input devices supported – mouse, joystick or keyboard – and whether they are a requirement or an option.

If you're unsure of the exact specification of your PC, look in its manual or contact the shop you bought it from. Take the details with you when you buy.

If it's raining outside, you can sit down with your PC and play golf with Arnold Palmer on a stunning recreation of the Old Course at St. Andrews. With wet grass and fog as options, Links LS 2001 is very realistic.

Sports games have always been popular with PC gamers. Perhaps they give the player a chance at sporting glory that they wouldn't otherwise have. Very few sports have been ignored by the computer games makers. You can play everything from football, golf and pool to Formula 1 motor racing.

Some games are more successful in their transfer to the PC than others. Golf and pool work well, but team games such as football and ice hockey are a little trickier to master. Some strive hard to achieve high levels of realism. In *Colin McRae Rally*, for example, you can tweak almost every aspect of your car's set-up to shave crucial tenths of a second off your time.

One of the best aspects of sports games for families is that, in many of them, two or more people can play at the same time. In a game such as golf, you

Movie tie-ins such as Harry Potter and the Sorcerer's Stone offer an immersive mix of adventure and puzzles.

can even set up and run your own family tournament.

There are PC games available for all ages, including the very young. Now even the pre-schooler can enjoy an interactive story or simple adventure with an educational element, such as *Oz: The Magical Adventure*. Slightly older children will enjoy titles based on familiar cartoon characters, such as any of the *Scooby-Doo* series, or elements from the toy cupboard, such as *Lego Soccer Mania*. These titles involve anything from solving various educational puzzles and challenges to playing games and taking part in activities. You may even be able to choose a skill level to match specific age groups. Many games aimed at children are designed to support specific National Curriculum Key Stages across a variety of topics.

● Plane speaking

If you dream of heading off into the wide blue yonder, flight simulators are ideal for taking to the skies while keeping your feet firmly on the ground. You can fly a large airliner across America, practise your landing technique in a Cessna 152, or streak across the skies at twice the speed of sound in the latest stealth fighter.

emotions with feature film tie-ins such as *Harry Potter and the Sorcerer's Stone*, combining action, adventure, humour and puzzle-solving.

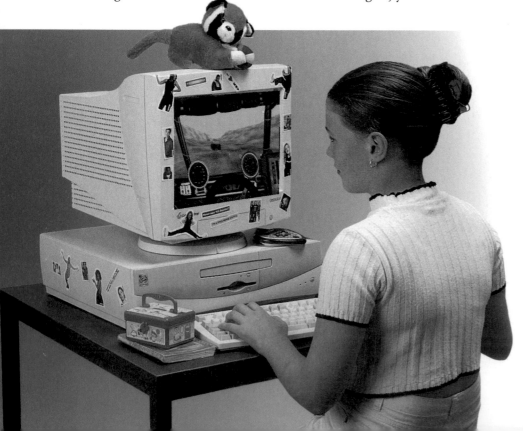

Programs such as the *Flight Simulator* series from Microsoft are unmatched for realism and detail – so much so that real pilots and trainees use them to practise their skills. If you crave a bit more excitement, then you might prefer to go for a combat flight simulator. These are just as detailed – one company making combat flight simulations also produces software for the RAF – and allow you to take part in complex missions simulating aspects of modern aerial warfare. It's pretty tricky to fly a plane and shoot things at the same time, but that's the challenge.

● Action heroes

There are also a huge number and variety of non-stop action games. In many, the focus is on fighting and shooting, but there are others that are more suitable for children. An action game doesn't have to be gory and titles such as *Monsters Inc: Scare Island* feature roughly similar gameplay to the likes of *Quake*, but with graphics and features aimed squarely at the

Tomb Raider's Lara Croft may have been gaming's first real heroine, but many modern titles such as Unreal II all feature women alongside the meatheads. These games also require more strategic thought than you first expect.

Not all online games involve big downloads and complex rules. The free games at the Cartoon Network Web site can be run directly inside a Web browser but still feature full animation, sound effects, music and great gameplay.

pre-teen market. Jumping across platforms and using Mike and Sully to scare robots is the order of the day, rather than slaughtering disgusting intergalactic mutants.

The most popular type of action game by far is the 'first person shoot-'em-up'. You run, jump, shoot and swim your way around detailed mazes, tunnels and buildings which are set in a 3D landscape. The aforementioned *Quake* series, *Unreal* and *Half-Life*, are the most popular 3D action games.

Kicking off with football games

Simple objectives, fast action and an infinite number of subtleties and strategies make football one of the best examples of the computer sports game.

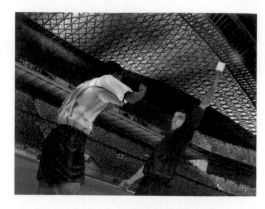

More than just a kickabout, 2002 FIFA World Cup forces you to contend with pressure from the crowd and strict referees.

As soon as programmers could make graphics move around a screen, they tried to reproduce the 'beautiful game' on a computer. And it's easy to see why: football is the most popular spectator sport in the world; it's fast, simple to understand and has a vast number of subtleties. Early PC versions of the game had only a passing resemblance to the real thing: one of the earliest, *International Soccer*, had only one player on each team (plus a goalie) and an almost two-dimensional pitch. Today, football games not only have whole teams, but 'motion-capture' from top players and the vocal talents of TV commentators such as John Motson and Barry Davies.

MANAGEMENT GAMES

Instead of relying on arcade skills, football-management games allow you to take on the role of a manager of a team – rather like the popular Fantasy Football games run by newspapers. Your task is to manage the finances of the club, buy and sell players and organize formations and match strategies – with the overall aim, of course, of winning the championship. These games can appear very slow and boring to non-football fans, but if you do enjoy football, you should be in seventh heaven. One of the most popular series in the genre is *FA Premier League Manager*. This appears in a new version each year.

The *FIFA* soccer series, published by Electronic Arts, is the most commercially successful football game in the world. It is updated once a year and is generally identified as simply *FIFA Soccer 2001*, *FIFA Soccer 2002* and so on. It has always been a huge seller, thanks largely to an official licence that grants the use of players' real names and faces. This means you can choose your favourite team, complete with requisite physical similarities and hairstyles. Although you can play against the computer, most fans prefer to play in two-player mode, since it gives you the advantage of 'proving' your team's superiority over that of a friend in a demonstrative, if virtual, fashion.

Before starting a match, you choose your team (either national or international) and variables such as the stadium, pitch type, weather conditions and so on. You must also select how long you wish to play a match for. Five or 10 minutes is a common option.

The on-pitch action in *FIFA* is typical of most modern 3D football games. When the game starts you see a portion of the pitch from an angle similar to that used in TV coverage and you are in control of the player closest to the ball. In theory you have control over the whole team, but in practice you control only one player at a time, and unless you choose otherwise it is always the player nearest to the ball. You move him around the pitch using the

The graphics in the FIFA games, by Electronic Arts, are the best of their kind. You can even make out their hairstyles!

Anco takes Player Manager **online as PlayAsManager, a subscription-based game which lets you control teams, replay key shots and analyse performance via the Internet.**

Premier League action is just the start: with Championship Manager, you interact with football governing bodies, the media, your board and expensive international transfers.

directional controls on a joystick or keypad and use a number of other buttons to kick, pass, run and shoot.

With the series now including *2002 FIFA World Cup*, the *FIFA* games have been generally regarded as the best football games for the PC as well as the most popular. You can

There's no interactive action in FA Premier League Manager, but you have full control over squads and the gameplay has strategic depth.

confidently expect new editions to appear not only for each local season but for each major tournament too, starting with Euro 2004.

● **Going into management**
One of the few games to deviate markedly from the standard *FIFA*-style approach to football games is the *Player Manager* series from Anco. Over the years these titles have been endorsed by big names in the sport, with the most recent being given the

full tagline *Alex Ferguson's Player Manager*. As you might expect, the game allows you to take the role of a player manager, thus giving you more control of overall tactics and strategy. Unfortunately, the action side of the game is not as refined as the *FIFA* titles, but the original approach to this crowded genre is quite refreshing.

Anco also offers a pay-to-play online variant of the game, known as *PlayAs Manager*. Here, you can take part in the entire 92-team league for the whole season, and you still benefit from 3D pitch and radar views, replays and ball-trace options.

Management-only type games are increasingly popular, and *FA Premier League Manager* mentioned opposite is just one of several on sale. For example, already into its 10th year and still going strong is *Championship Manager* from Eidos (the makers of *Tomb Raider*). Another annually updated title, this game has grown into one of the biggest of its kind, featuring detailed profiles for over 100,000 players, managers and coaches within 26 concurrent international leagues. This adds a new dimension to the genre, following official rules for match bans and player transfers, and even letting you issue ultimatums.

CONTACT POINTS

There is always a good spread of football games available, both action and management type, but particularly so when a big international tournament is about to take place. The following titles, though, have proven to be popular through the years and are updated on a regular basis to take account both of new player signings to teams in the world of real football and advances in the exciting virtual world of computer graphics technology.

FIFA Soccer 2002
Price £30*
2002 FIFA World Cup
Price: £35*
FA Premier League Manager 2002
Price: £25*
Electronic Arts
Tel: 01932 450 000
http://uk.ea.com

Alex Ferguson's Player Manager 2001
Price: £25*
Anco
Tel: 01322 292 513
www.anco.co.uk

Championship Manager 01/02
Price: £30*
Eidos Interactive
Tel: 0870 9000 222
www.eidosinteractive.co.uk

* UK prices

Mind games

The qualities that make board games, such as chess and backgammon, so enduringly popular have been successfully transferred to mind – or strategy – games on the computer. To overcome the challenge of your opponent, be it another player or the PC itself, you need skill, forethought and good powers of concentration.

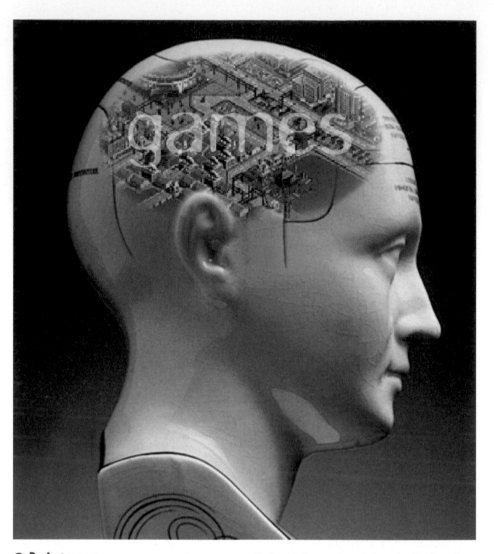

Mind games have been played on computers ever since the first programmers created draughts and chess games. Today's top chess programs can beat Grand Masters, but less daunting mind games are available for the rest of us. They don't involve any of the violence that is found in the shooting and fighting games, there are no car chases, explosions or aircraft dog-fights, but they can be just as exciting.

● A new classic

As well as classic games such as chess and backgammon, there are now more and more commercial games being converted for you to play on your home computer. Based on the hit TV quiz show, *The Weakest Link* has the music, the format and even the scary Anne Robinson as host. This is excellent entertainment for the whole family as up to seven contestants can play at one time.

● Brain teasers

For a different challenge, you can tackle one of the many puzzle games developed for people with leisure time to spend in front of their PC.

Computer mind games aren't so much about beating an opponent, but defeating your powerful computer. And beware – these games can be incredibly absorbing. You may intend to play for just 20 minutes, but find that several hours have elapsed by the time you finally concede defeat, or triumph over your PC.

Brain Teasing Games from GSP offers 25 different games giving you hours of challenging fun as you try to get your head round these mind boggling puzzles. Poker, Safe Cracker, Thinker and Klondike are just a few of the brain teasers featured.

Also from GSP is *PC Guide Editors Choice Mind Games* – a highly recommended CD-ROM with a wide selection of great games which include something for everyone. There are no

The best mind games give your brain a real workout. Not only do they provide all the challenges and excitement of competition, they can open doors of discovery to whole areas of knowledge.

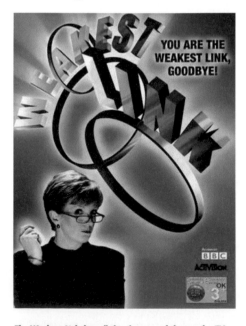

The Weakest Link has all the elements of the popular TV quiz show of the same name.

Assess your leadership potential with Civilization: Call To Power II. You must guide your tribe from the stone age to the space age using skill, courage and ingenuity.

Building an empire requires careful consideration of many socio-economic aspects, including diplomacy, politics, culture, trade and even war.

time limits so you can keep on playing for as long as you like to improve your score and there is also a useful browser to simplify the process of selecting and installing each game.

● World domination

For those who want more action and a different type of challenge, there is a wide range of global strategy games. The board based forerunner of this game type was *Risk*, where players tried to conquer the world by military means alone and success or failure rested on the roll of a dice. However, much more than luck is needed if you are to succeed in the latest global strategy games.

CONTACT POINTS

The Weakest Link
Price: £9.99*
Civilization: Call to Power II
Price: £5.99*
Return to Castle Wolfenstein
Price: £19.99*
Activision
Tel: 01753 756 100
www.activision.com

**Brain Teasing Games
PC Guide Editors Choice Mind Games**
Price of each: £9.99*
GSP
Tel: 01480 496 666
www.gsp.cc

*UK Prices

A popular one is *Civilization: Call To Power II*, in which you begin as the leader of a primitive tribe and your challenge is to guide them in a quest to dominate the world and conquer space.

This fascinating game covers a 6,300-year time span, from primitive history to the future realms of science fiction. Help your people to explore the world, build armies, defeat rival civilizations and form strategic alliances with other powerful nations. You can also research new leaps in technology, starting with basics, such as the wheel. Then you graduate to choosing forms of government, such as a republic or monarchy, and move on to mass production, recycling and even space travel.

To be successful at the game, the decisions you take must be wise ones based on all the knowledge you have accumulated – the game does not work on just a random basis. These types of strategy game are a great way to encourage reluctant young students to start learning about what makes society work.

● Fight against evil forces

Return to Castle Wolfenstein from Activision is set during the Second World War and features the demonic Heinrich Himmler and his evil lieutenant, Death's Head. Through genetic engineering and using occult powers, Himmler is trying to raise an unstoppable army to conquer the world. Your task is to

escape from the castle where Himmler is dabbling in the black arts, report his activities to the world at large, then return to thwart his plans. The surroundings are dangerous and hostile including hidden crypts, air bases, secret weapons facilities and genetic labs. The game can be played in single or multiplayer mode and features outstanding graphics – be careful or you might get hooked!

SITES TO @ VISIT

Mind games are exceptionally popular on the Internet. Many of the games mentioned here either include Internet options or are available in special multi-player versions.

Internet Chess Club
Chess is popular around the globe and you can find world-wide opponents at:
www.chessclub.com/

Shockwave
This site offers a vast range of games from action and sport to jigsaws and puzzles:
www.shockwave.com/

MPOG.COM
If you want to play a game involving several other players, check out the online multi-player directory:
www.mpog.com/

The Internet

Introducing the Internet

The Internet lets you travel around the globe at the click of your mouse. Step on to the information superhighway and discover how your PC can give you a window looking out over the whole world.

There is something on the Internet for everybody – not just businessmen and academics. From your home, you can connect to millions of other computers all over the world and find information about almost any subject you want.

The Internet is a worldwide network of computers linked together by high-speed cables. There are millions of computers making up this information superhighway – some the size of a small building, others the same size and type as your home PC. This means that anyone with a PC and a modem can become part of the Internet by connecting through an ordinary telephone line (many homes can also connect to the Internet via cable TV or digital telephone lines for high-speed surfing).

Once you're connected, the real power and interest of the Internet becomes apparent. This huge network of computers is as easy to use as your own PC. Just as you click your way around the programs and files on your computer with Windows, the Internet lets you click your way around this worldwide information network.

● **Something for everyone**
There are computers (or Internet sites) that cover every subject imaginable: celebrities and entertainment, sport, news, science and much more. You'll find text, sound, pictures and even video clips.

You can subscribe to discussion groups and participate in debates with thousands of like-minded people around the world. Many of these groups have specific interests, with well over 10,000 different topics covered.

● **Email for free**
Email (or electronic mail) is the fastest way to communicate with the millions of other users on the Internet. You can send letters and files from your PC without the cost of a stamp and it's almost instantaneous – you can often receive a reply from the other side of the world within minutes.

● **Just browsing**
The World Wide Web is the name for the network of links that connects all the different Internet sites. It is probably the most popular part of the Net. With a browser, you can use the World Wide Web to access information on the Internet.

INTERNET ORIGINS

Although it has only recently been available to the general public, the Internet has existed since the late 1960s. It was originally designed by the US military as a way of protecting its main computer facilities in the event of a nuclear attack. With the advent of the World Wide Web in 1989, the Internet became so flexible that almost anyone in the world could connect his or her computer to the system.

Exploring the World Wide Web

The Web is huge – hundreds of thousands of places to visit and every interest under the sun catered for. It's as diverse as the world itself.

INFORMATION on anything you care to name is available on the World Wide Web. To help you find it, easy-to-use Web searching tools will find the sites covering subjects you're interested in. The search tools are not programs that you need to buy and install on your computer, they are special Web sites themselves. Once your computer's modem is plugged into the telephone line and set up, and you have selected an Internet service provider (we'll explain what these are on pages 138–139), you can log on to them as you wish.

Web sites are made up of interactive pages; you click on a link and something happens – you might jump to a new page, start a video clip or hear a sound recording.

Instead of starting on page one and reading to the end, as you do with most books, with a Web site you jump back and forward as your interest takes you. Many sites don't look like book pages at all; some have amazing 3D worlds to explore. Here are some of the types of Web site you will be able to browse when your PC is on the information superhighway.

SHOPPING

This is the site of Innovations, the high street and catalogue retailer – http://www.innovations.co.uk/. You can view the catalogue and place your order online. Simply click on the items you want, review the final details on the order form, then another mouse click instantly sends your order.

Click on one of these boxes at the top to select a category from the Innovations catalogue.

THE Internet is becoming the largest superstore ever, stocking virtually anything you could want to buy. You can visit your favourite store or browse through online shopping centres, which bring together shops selling a wide range of goods and services.

You can order almost anything that takes your fancy from the thousands of online shops using your credit card. It will then be delivered to your home.

NEWS

OFFERING unparalleled access to world news and current affairs, the Internet lets you keep up with the latest stories as they happen.

Newspapers from around the world are available online, and TV news services, such as CNN (Cable News Network) and Sky TV, also offer excellent coverage.

There are even special interest news sites, including some designed especially for children to enjoy.

News from all over the world can be picked up almost as soon as it happens. The CNN site – http://www.cnn.com – divides all news up into key categories, such as world news, European news, world weather and so on. This is the European news page (http://europe.cnn.com/).

This link takes you to the story behind the headline in full. Or, if you want to see a larger version of the picture, just click on it.

WHATEVER your favourite sport, it is likely to have at least one devoted fan who has prepared a Web site dedicated to it. By visiting the site, you can pick up the latest news and gossip, and chat to other fans around the world.

As you might expect, football fans are well catered for on the Web, with a mass of information on famous teams, league positions, fixtures and player profiles.

A motor racing fan can go straight to the official Ferrari site – http://www.ferrari.it – and get the inside track on the team. One of the best things about sports sites is that they are updated frequently.

Become part of the Ferrari community – this link enables you to chat with the team.

This link will take you to the shop where official merchandise can be purchased.

A very popular site is that of the television show *Friends* – http://www.nbc.com/friends. Here you can discover everything you wanted to know about the show and its stars.

Click here to find out more about the show and its history.

To read the biographies of your favourite stars of the show, click on this link.

KEEPING up with your favourite band, finding out about exhibitions or simply organizing your TV viewing is easy on the Web. Major TV companies have their own sites where you can find a wealth of information on TV shows and the antics of your favourite celebrities.

If you want to find a restaurant, see a movie, or find out about an interesting new bar, you will find the Internet a great resource.

YOU can study for school or college and even obtain a degree using the Internet. Universities from around the world have sites and some offer online courses.

Most schools now have an Internet connection and many schoolchildren use it for research and for keeping in touch with schools abroad. Children can also visit special online exhibitions created by world famous museums.

Whatever the homework assignment, there's a museum or education site to help out. Here, The Natural History Museum – http://www.nhm.ac.uk – has a educational activity site.

Click on this link to view other sites on natural history.

The education site has something for everybody, and caters for the needs of both adults and children.

What makes a Web site special?

A Web site can combine text, pictures, sound and even video, all connected by links for easy navigation through its pages. Here's a tour around a typical Web site to show the depth of information available.

Home page ▶

Every Web site has a home page, rather like the contents page of a magazine or book, which contains **hyperlinks** to other pages of information on the site.

The Web site has its own unique address on the Internet, which will look something like: http://www.spurs.co.uk. You simply type this address into your Web browser to go to that site. If you see a link on a page, you don't even need to type an address, just click on it.

Multimedia ▼

Web sites need not look like static magazine pages – many sites have video and sound clips. This site even has audio and visual interviews with various Spurs players. Simply click on the link and the video will play.

Text ▼

A good Web site is more than just lots of pictures and hyperlinks. It can be jam-packed with in-depth articles and features – there are no paper costs to worry about, after all. The Spurs site has lots of information on the players, the club's history, statistics and forthcoming events.

Downloads ▶

Many sites have images that you can download to your PC. The Spurs site has a selection of screensavers and wallpaper to choose from. Once you have made your selection your computer will download the relevant installer on to your machine. To activate the installer, double-click on the installer icon and it will then install the image on to your computer.

Forms ▶

Some Web pages are designed as simple forms. Here you can type in any suggestions for features that you would like to see on the site, and opt to receive emails and information relating to Tottenham Hotspur FC.

Interactivity ▲

Some Web sites hardly look like their paper-based equivalents. This visual tour of the Spurs ground White Hart Lane works just as if it were a computer program running on your PC. You can zoom in and out, and have a 360° view of the pitch. All this is achieved using the powerful computer you are accessing.

Advertising banner ▶

Many Web sites carry advertising. If you want to go to the advertiser's site, just click on the banner.

Email ▶

Some links on a Web page are for sending email. An email address looks something like: name@place.com (the @ symbol is pronounced 'at'). Click on an email address and your Internet email program will start, ready for you to type your message.

WHAT IT MEANS

HYPERLINKS

Hyperlinks, or links, are the most important part of the World Wide Web. These are items you can click on to move to another page. The Web site designer can make a site as interactive as necessary using hyperlinks.

Some hyperlinks look like underlined text of a different colour, often blue. Links can also be part of, or all of, a picture, or small buttons like the icons in Windows. You can tell which parts of the page are links because the normal mouse pointer changes to a pointing hand when it passes over them.

What you need to get on the Internet

You want to get on the information superhighway, but you're not sure where to begin and you're afraid of the cost. Here's our easy guide to what you need to get connected and how to minimize those Internet expenses.

Don't worry if it seems like the rest of the world is on the Internet and you've been left behind. Internet users are only a small, but rapidly growing, group of people. Over the next few pages, we're going to tackle the two major obstacles that stop people becoming part of the Internet community: the jargon, and the thing that puts a lot of people off, the cost.

On pages 138–139, we'll look at how expensive it is to get online and how much it costs to stay connected. We'll also give you tips on how to keep the telephone line costs down.

A modem and Internet connection will open interesting doors all around the world for you and your family, including news, games, sport and email. Every day Internet access is becoming easier, quicker and less expensive.

WHAT IT MEANS

BIT

Short for binary digit, the bit is the smallest unit of information on your PC. Every piece of information computers use and store is converted into a sequence of bits. For example, there are 8 bits in a byte and a CD-ROM contains over 650 million bytes, or more than 5,200,000,000 bits.

First, though, let's tackle the question of what type of equipment you'll need to get started.

● Essential equipment

The essentials are a computer and a telephone line – you probably already have these – and a modem. A modem is a device that can send and receive computer data through the telephone line. Your PC will most likely arrive with a built-in modem card (see page 92) but older models had external modems which connect to a port at the back of the computer. Check the documents that came with your PC.

If you don't have a modem, you can add one to your PC very easily.

The most important consideration when choosing a modem is the speed at which it can send and receive data. This is usually measured in bits per second (bps). The higher the value, the faster the modem, and the faster it operates, the shorter the time you need to spend online – and the cheaper your telephone bills.

Most of today's modems that operate with a normal telephone line

If you've got a telephone, you've got a route to the Internet. With a special device, called a modem, your computer connects straight to a normal telephone socket.

Page ① ② ③ ④ ⑤ ⑥ ⑦

Fake tans are shaking off their streaky orange image. We've found some that converted even the most sceptical to the joy of going bronze without the risk of harm from the sun

Best Buy Guide

Most of the products in our trial gave a decent tan, but we found a clear winner in the women's test - **Sainsbury's Moisturising Self-Tanning Lotion** (£4.99 for 200ml), which was also one of the cheapest. Our volunteers found it convenient to use and it produced a good, even colour. Ambre Solaire, Avon and Clinique did well, too. Clarins, Lancaster and Lancôme gave a reasonable tan but they were more expensive, costing more than four times as much

The Which? online service (www.which.net) includes detailed consumer information on a wide range of topics featured in its monthly publication.

Virgin Net (www.virgin.net) is entertainment orientated with a play finder, movie finder and gig guide.

run at 56,000bps, with older ones operating at 33,600bps or even 28,800bps. Modems are relatively cheap, and it always pays to get the fastest available.

● At your service

To connect to the Internet you will need to join an Internet service provider (ISP) – an organization that has computers permanently attached to the Internet. When you want to go online, your PC uses your modem to contact their computers and you become part of the Internet world.

Traditionally, ISPs all used to be specialized companies charging you a monthly fee (typically, £10–12) to use their service. Some simply provided software, a connection to the Internet and an email service. But others – such as AOL – supplied organized content and services, at a slightly higher price. You decided if you just wanted a means of diving into the Internet or whether you preferred the

more structured experience offered by these online services.

But as both the PC and the Internet have become much more of a mass-market phenomenon, a large number of free ISPs have sprung up, many of them backed by major high-street retailers. The first of these was Freeserve, which was set up by electrical store Dixons, and very quickly WH Smith, BT, Tesco and a number of national newspapers followed suit. Similarly, the distinction between an ISP pure and simple, and an online service has been eroded; nowadays, most ISPs

themselves provide some sort of news, entertainment and shopping service at their own Web site. On pages 138–139 we'll take a look at some of the different ISPs, the sort of content each offers, and the pros and cons of a free service versus a subscription based provider.

● Name and number

You sign up for a service either by using your PC and modem to dial the ISP's number and following the instructions on screen, or by installing the necessary software from a CD which you can collect from a shop or have sent to you. When connecting to some ISPs you might have to enter your credit card details for billing.

The most important aspects to consider when you sign up are your user name and your password. Your user name is the name you will have on the Internet and which people use to send you email. Choose a name carefully (beware of joke names you might regret later) and have some alternatives ready in case your preferred name is already taken.

Keep your password secret – anyone who knows it could use your account and peek at your private email. Your ISP – whether free or paid for – will also provide you with a suite of Internet software, although of course, Windows XP comes with an email program and a World Wide Web browser.

UK Online is a family orientated site – you can set up a children's account, which provides your children with selective and screened Internet access.

Tiscali (www.tiscali.co.uk) contains lots of current news, sport and entertainment from UK-based sources. It also includes links to other Web sites that may be of interest.

Which ISP?

Here we take a look at some of the different types of Internet service providers that are available – and the real costs involved.

ONCE YOU'VE decided to go online, you have to choose an ISP. There are dozens of ISPs and several different types of service to choose from. Choosing the right one is mainly a matter of selecting one which offers what you want at the right price.

Fortunately, almost all ISPs offer the same set of basic services: Internet access, an email address and some Web space for your own Web pages. A few offer more, such as extra email addresses. However, the price you pay even for very similar packages can vary significantly, and it's important to match your family's surfing needs with the charging scheme to get best value for money.

● Online costs

The costs of surfing come in two forms – telephone call charges and ISP subscription charges. Some ISPs make no monthly subscription charge at all. Instead they take a commission from each telephone charge you incur when you go online; these telephone charges are typically the same price as a local call. These are often called free ISPs. This type of service best suits someone who goes online for a few short periods.

Other ISPs offer freephone access instead, which does away with the first element, leaving you with just a fixed monthly charge to pay (typically £10–16) no matter how long you stay online. This is perfect for families who want to limit online costs. Some ISPs offer a choice of these two packages, so you can pick the one you want when you register.

Visit www.net4nowt.com for a listing of ISPs. A few ISP services incur both types of costs. However, these are generally aimed at business users, with improved levels of service, and the charging system rarely suits home users.

● Paying for help?

One other important aspect of the ISP package is the part you hope you never have to use – the help line.

There are several sites which list ISPs and their services, such as www.net4nowt.com, so do a little research before signing up.

If things go wrong – your Internet connection stops working, or email messages are being lost – you may need to contact the ISP's technical support help line.

Some ISPs use a premium rate help-line number, which typically costs 50p per minute, although can be up to £1 per minute. To match the cost of a £10 subscription, you would have to make 20 minutes of support phone calls a month.

How significant this cost is to you depends on how confident you are at setting up and running the necessary software on your own. Internet software is much more stable now than in the early days, and we give you step-by-step guidance on installing and using two ISPs on pages 140–149.

● Online costs

The cost of technical support is not the only issue to take into account. There's also the question of what kind of ISP you want. Many ISPs offer a selection of Internet content on their home pages. Freeserve, for example, offers up-to-the-minute news, entertainment stories and a selection of links to home shopping services. Those ISPs known as 'online service providers' (see AOL, below) offer an even more structured approach to the Internet, together with specialized content you can only access by subscribing as a member.

If you decide to sign up with a free ISP, you should remember to keep the account active; most free services retain the right to terminate your account if you do not use it for a 90-day period. This may never happen, but if you are a paying customer you can be pretty sure that your ISP is not going to cut you off for non-usage.

Finally, whichever ISP you choose, remember that you can always change it if you find the service unsatisfactory; you just download and install new software. To avoid having to change your email address when you do this, see pages 154–157.

AOL

AOL is one of the biggest ISPs in the world. It has around 34 million users world-wide, with 1.7 million or so in the UK. AOL provides a different approach to most ISPs. Its service gives you a structured approach to the Internet, providing 'channels' with content related to particular subject areas. Much of the content is unavailable elsewhere, which explains why it is a subscription service. AOL charges a fixed fee per month, which includes telephone charges – AOL has a freephone dial-up number, so you don't have any extra phone call charges to pay. There is also a freephone help line for members.

One of the many channels featured on AOL.

Freeserve

http://www.freeserve.com

Freeserve was the first of the UK's free ISPs and has amassed more than one million registrations. It's backed by high street electrical store Dixons and supplies all the services you would expect: Internet browsing, email addresses and Web space for your own site. Freeserve's home page provides structured and unfussy access to UK-related news, sport and entertainment content.

BTopenworld

http://www.btopenworld.com

As you would expect, BT has a cutting edge presence on the Web. Its home page offers a wealth of information, allowing users to personalise their own web page and access information including world news, sport updates, weather reports and the latest jobs 24 hours a day.

Demon

http://www.demon.net

Demon is a subscription Internet service provider that has some news and shopping content, but a large part of its site is aimed at business Internet users. It contains links to Web hosting and dedicated Internet connection – or leased line – services.

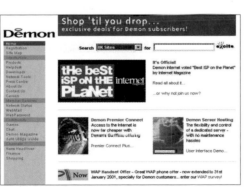

Tesco

http://www.tesco.com

This is another free ISP – but you have to have a Tesco club card to join up. The home page is bright and breezy and, as you might expect from a supermarket chain, the site is strong on online shopping. You can check out your club card points online too.

Reader's Digest

http://www.rdplus.net

Rdplus.net is Reader's Digest's own free ISP. It gives users instant access to Reader's Digest's own Web pages, where you can play games, laugh at jokes, enter competitions, shop to your heart's content and gain valuable hints and tips from the worlds of Gardening and DIY. Finding your way around is made easy by the pages' open, friendly look.

PC TIPS

Keep your bills down

• Ensure your ISP supplies connection numbers charged at local call rates.

• Try to plan the time you go online. The cheapest time is generally at weekends (midnight Friday to midnight Sunday) – the BT local call rate then is 1p per minute. This rises to 1.5p per minute at off-peak times (after 6pm weekdays) and 4p per minute at peak times (8am to 6pm weekdays), although this may vary with different telephone service providers.

• Add your ISP's connection number to money-saving schemes operated by your phone company (for example, BT's Friends and Family).

• Avoid times when Internet use is highest, because Web pages take longer to download, meaning increased phone bills. For example, the Internet is faster before America wakes up, so for better results you should connect before 2pm in the UK, which is 9am in New York City.

Setting up a modem

Most home users use a modem to connect their PCs to the Internet. You can use Windows to check your modem and make sure it's set up for economical surfing.

A modem is a device that connects your PC to the telephone network, and, therefore, potentially to any other computer that is also connected to the telephone network, anywhere in the world.

Many newer home PCs already have a modem, but you may have overlooked it as some are built into the computer's system unit (see Hardware p90-93). You can use Windows to check to see if you have a modem and that it is working correctly. All you then need to do is connect it to your telephone line.

● Plug in and go

It is easy to plug your modem into your existing phone line using a 'splitter' plug, which works much like the adaptor you use to plug two appliances into an electrical socket. Modems come with quite long leads, and this might result in long cables trailing from the nearest socket to the desk where you keep your computer. If this is the case, you might need to think about installing an extra telephone socket – either by using a DIY kit or getting your telephone company to put one in.

Remember, if you only have one telephone line, you can't make telephone calls while you are using the Internet, so it could be worth thinking about getting an extra phone line.

A simple splitter plug lets you plug the modem into your telephone socket alongside your existing telephone.

Modems can be external to the PC, as shown here, or fitted inside the main cabinet. Internally fitted ones are neater, needing far less cabling.

● Choosing a modem

If your PC doesn't have a modem, you can add one for around £30-40. All modern modems operate at the same speed – which is 56,000 bits per second (bps) – and have the same basic features, allowing you to use them to connect to other computers – for Web surfing – and to work as fax machines – sending and receiving faxes. The more expensive modems often include software that lets your PC work as an answering machine, or extra hardware features. Internal modems require you to open up the PC and fit the small circuit board – a potentially risky procedure for novice computer users. For this reason, most home users opt for an external modem that simply plugs into one of the sockets on the back of the PC.

HOW YOUR MODEM WORKS

A modem works by converting the digital information that a computer deals with into an analogue signal that can be sent down the phone line. It 'modulates' data going into the phone network so it becomes a series of whistles and bleeps, and 'demodulates' the signal coming out back into digital bits – hence the name 'modem', which is short for MOdulate/DEModulate.

Configuring your modem

Use Windows to check that your modem is correctly installed and that it automatically disconnects when you have finished your surfing sessions.

1 To see if your PC already has an internal modem installed, and to check that it's ready to use, use the Windows Control Panel. First, click on the Start button and then select the Control Panel entry from the menu.

2 When the Control Panel window appears, double-click on the Phone and Modem Options icon.

3 In the Phone and Modem Options dialog box, click on the Modems tab. If your modem is correctly installed, it is listed in the central panel. Select it and click on the Properties button.

4 The next dialog box confirms that the device is working properly. If you have a modem that Windows tells you is not working properly, click the Troubleshoot button to try to fix the problem.

5 If your modem is working properly, close the dialog boxes to return to the Control Panel. Now you can check that Windows is set up to automatically disconnect your modem from the Internet when you have finished surfing. Start by double-clicking the Internet Options icon in the Control Panel.

6 In the Internet Properties dialog box, click on the Connections tab and select the connection to your Internet service provider (ISP). Then click the Settings button.

7 When the Settings dialog box opens, click the Advanced button near the bottom of the dialog box.

8 This opens up a small dialog box that lets you change the way your ISP connection uses your modem. First, use the third option to adjust the amount of idle time that Windows waits before disconnecting. Make sure that the fourth option is ticked – this automatically disconnects your modem from the Internet when you close your Internet programs.

WHEN YOUR PC CAN'T FIND YOUR MODEM

If you know your PC has a modem, but it doesn't appear in the Phone and Modem Options dialog box (see Step 3), it is not correctly installed. If it's one you have installed yourself, it may not be correctly connected – retrace the steps given in the modem manual and double-check all cable connections. If it was supplied new with your PC, contact your PC dealer for support – there's a chance that it needs extra software to work with Windows XP.

Connecting to Freeserve

Getting onto the Internet might seem daunting, but it's really easy. Most Internet service providers, including Freeserve, supply all the software you need on a CD-ROM.

To access the Internet you need to sign up with an Internet service provider (ISP). As we've seen, there are many around (see pages 136–137), ranging from those that are entirely free, to those which charge a monthly subscription. Whichever you choose, the process of installing the software and getting connected will be similar. On the next few pages we'll take a detailed look at how to set up an account with Freeserve, the UK's first and the biggest ISP.

Freeserve has several types of package, ranging from a free ISP deal called No Ties (where you pay only for phone calls) to fixed-cost monthly subscriptions, with names such as AnyTime and HomeTime. At the time of going to press, the Freeserve CD only covered a promotional offer for AnyTime (see Getting the Freeserve CD, right). If you're already online – perhaps with another ISP – you don't need the CD-ROM. You can sign up directly by visiting the Freeserve Web site and following the Join Freeserve links. These online sign-up pages help to increase the competition and decrease prices. Later in the course, we'll show you how to change ISP online.

● What you need
The CD contains two main bits of software to install on your PC. The first is the browser software that lets you navigate the Internet and view Web sites. Freeserve supplies the latest version of Microsoft's Internet Explorer, but if you want to you can change at a later date to its main rival, Netscape Navigator. The second element is software that lets you compose, send and receive email. The Freeserve CD installs the latest version of Microsoft's Outlook Express (which may be more up-to-date than the one already installed on your PC).

GETTING THE FREESERVE CD

Freeserve was originally launched by Dixons and you can pick up a free sign-up CD-ROM from the Dixons range of shops, which include Currys, PC World and The Link. The competitive nature of the ISP business means that the offers and types of packages change frequently, so it's worth looking out for special promotional deals – just don't choose the first one you find.

Exploring Freeserve

After installing the Freeserve software, click on its Desktop icon to connect to the Internet and visit Freeserve's home page.

❶ Click here if you're having problems and you will be sent to Freeserve's online help area, which includes a Q&A section.

❷ A search engine is a means of looking for information – crucial on the Internet. Freeserve has its own search engine – just type a significant word in the Search box, click on the Go icon and the search engine will provide a list of sites that fit the bill. You can also use French or Spanish search engines by clicking on the foreign links at the very bottom of the page but you will need to know the language.

❹ Like many ISPs, Freeserve selects and organizes Internet information for you into a number of 'channels' – themed areas of content. Just click on any of the items under the Channels heading near the top of the page and you'll get a listing of what's in each separate channel. This saves you the trouble of seeking out a multitude of separate Web sites – but there's nothing to stop you going off to explore.

❸ Online shopping is strongly supported on Freeserve. You can buy anything from a holiday to an electric toaster.

❺ Freeserve's home page contains different news stories each day. Just click on the link after each item to get the full story downloaded to you.

Entering new worlds

Freeserve helps you make a start on the Internet with its selection of categories catering for a range of interests.

A virtual supermarket

Freeserve gives you plenty of opportunities to get involved in the boom area of online shopping. Click on the shopping link on the home page and you'll be offered the choice to buy a wide range of goods, from furniture to electrical goods and from books, music and computer CDs to travel and holiday home swaps. There are also some great last-minute bargains to be had. To shop online your credit or debit card details will be required. There's no real safety concern here as nearly all online merchants use secure encryption software. The chances of a fraudulent transaction occurring are much the same as when buying goods via the telephone.

That's entertainment

Freeserve's selected content is strong on what's happening in the world of showbiz. Headline stories feature the latest news on personalities from TV, film and music. Click on the links to see the full details, often with photographs. Elsewhere on Freeserve you'll get all the news on the latest music releases, while the Television and Radio areas supply details of home entertainment possibilities.

World of sport

You can find out about all kinds of sports on Freeserve, but football receives top line prominence. There are regularly updated headlines on the home page and one click takes you to the stories behind them. You'll also find interviews, the latest gossip and rumours, and a selection of links to get you updated with your own team's news.

Beat the exam blues

Children taking GCSE exams or Key Stage tests in the UK might well be grateful for the revision pages in Freeserve's Learning area. Topics covered include Maths, English and Science from Key Stage 2 through to GCSE. General tips on revising and taking exams (and advice for parents) are backed up with a wealth of information and self-test pages. With the Internet, revision is a great deal more appealing.

INTERNET USE BY KIDS

There are certain to be sites on the Internet that you would not want your children to see. Also, you don't want them to be generating massive phone bills. Freeserve doesn't supply an Internet monitoring service, but there are third-party programs that give you a measure of control. One such program, Net Nanny, has joined forces with Freeserve. You can find out more at the Net Nanny site, www.netnanny.com

Installing Freeserve software and signing up

The Freeserve CD does just about everything for you. Once you've installed the software and registered as a new account, you have the same Internet access and benefits as are offered by most ISPs.

1 Put the CD-ROM in the CD drive. The software will start automatically. It will check your PC to see that Freeserve isn't already installed, then open the first screen. Click the Install button to continue. If you encounter problems, you can click on the Help button (see Getting Help, opposite).

2 Once you have clicked on the Install button, the connection wizard window appears to guide you through the process. If you don't have the most recent version of Internet Explorer and Outlook Express, then Freeserve will install them for you. To install any of the software you will be required to read and accept the License Agreement. Select the I accept the agreement option and then click Next. Now you'll see a screen giving details of the installation progress. This can take a few minutes, as there's a lot of data to transfer to your hard disk.

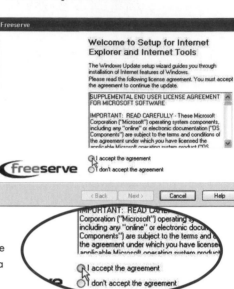

3 You are warned to save any files you may have open because Windows is going to restart your computer to complete the installation procedure. Click on the Finish button. The main screen reappears but wait until the computer restarts automatically.

4 When Windows restarts your PC at the end of the software installation, a window will appear telling you that it is updating your system settings. This makes start-up rather slower than usual. When the Desktop reappears, you'll see that there are two shortcuts on your Desktop: one to Freeserve Internet and one to Freeserve Help. Once you've signed up (see Steps 7–14), all you'll have to do to connect to Freeserve and the Internet is double-click on the first of these icons.

5 After the restart, the program presents the Internet packages available. This particular CD contains an AnyTime special offer, but you may be offered a choice of packages. Click the Register button for the package you want.

6 Freeserve connects to the Internet as the next stages are all completed on-line to register your details and new settings. The Internet Connection Wizard will start by dialling up to Freeserve.

7 The Registration Introduction screen gives you lots of information about what will happen during registration plus support phone numbers. Make a note of these in case you need them later.

SHORTCUTS

When installing Freeserve you lose your Taskbar as the installation process fills the screen. To access your Desktop, press [Ctrl]+[Esc].

8 The next window displays Freeserve's Terms of Use – in effect, its terms and conditions. When you have made yourself aware of these, click I Accept to continue.

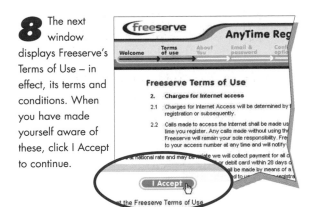

9 After a short pause, the Personal Information screen comes up. Fill in all the relevant areas, either by moving your mouse cursor to the boxes and clicking before typing, or by using the [Tab] key to jump from box to box. In some boxes you can select an answer from the drop-down menus.

10 A screen containing advice about choosing an email address now appears. This is a step which requires a little thought: once you've used an email address for a while you will not want to change it, so choose an email address you're happy with from the start. Freeserve has around 1.5 million accounts in the UK and a lot of the more desirable email addresses have already been taken. You can choose something unusual or be prepared to try a few times when the software tells you the name you've chosen is already in use. If you want something related to your family name, you might well have to settle for the name followed by a number. Click Continue on the advice screen.

GETTING HELP

Like many ISPs, Freeserve's free or low-cost access deals don't include free telephone technical help. This is generally charged at around 50p per minute, or more, so you only use it when in extreme difficulty. Try other options first. The Freeserve installation disc, for example, has an extensive Help file which is quite likely to contain the

solution you need. If you're able to connect then you can also browse the Q&A section on the Freeserve site (see Exploring Freeserve, on page 142). In addition, Freeserve offers a free technical help email service: send your query to the help desk and they'll mail you back with possible diagnoses and cures.

11 Now type in a password; you will be asked to re-enter this as confirmation. Choose a password that's easy for you to remember but that is unlikely to be guessed by anybody else. Click on Continue.

12 The next screen is your Account details summary. Although Windows automatically remembers your details, you should make a note of them or print the page as you may need to use them in the future.

13 Depending on the CD you are using, you may need to confirm the Internet package and type in a promotions code. If you have opted for a subscriptions-based package, you'll need to enter your credit card details on the subsequent page.

14 Click on the Finish button send all your information through and finalize your connections. In future, just double-click the shortcut on your PC Desktop. You'll see the Dial-up Connection window with your account details already entered. Click Connect to complete the connection to Freeserve.

Connecting to AOL

AOL is the world's largest online service. Here, we show you what you can expect to find if you join, how easy it is to connect for the first time and where you can get the AOL software.

The initials AOL stand for America Online. Despite the name, it's a global Internet service provider – with more than 34 million members – that supplies a lot of exclusive online content and services for its subscribers.

This members-only service also provides Internet email – so you can keep in touch with other Internet users. To connect to the Internet and World Wide Web, you use the customized Web browser which is included in the AOL package.

● One-button browsing

AOL aims to make it simple for non-expert users to get on the Internet. To access the Internet via AOL, all you do is click on the Internet button and then choose the option you want from the next screen. You can browse the Web, download files, access newsgroups and more besides. There's even space for you to build your own Web pages.

The AOL service is split into 23 different subject areas (or channels); these include House and Home, Parenting, Travel, Technology, Your Money, Entertainment, News and Weather, Sport, Games, Local Life and Kids. Every channel also has a Chat area where you can have live online conversations with other AOL

The floating AOL channel screens are designed to make the service easy and fun to use, and you can have several open at a time. The blue menu bars running along the top of the screen provide access to other areas of AOL's service.

users. On pages 148–149, we take a look at some of these areas in more detail and give examples of what AOL has to offer.

● Try before you buy

Internet service providers compete very fiercely, so the good news is that you can try out the AOL service before committing yourself. You'll need to get a copy of the AOL software, but AOL will send you a free CD-ROM (see Try an AOL free trial, right). Of course, you'll need a modem so that you can connect to AOL through your phone line.

You then need to work through the setup program. Opposite, we show you how to get connected for the first time. The process is the same whether you download the software or get it on disk. Once you're signed up, you'll have full access to AOL's complete range of services.

Click on AOL's Internet tab to help banish the mystery and uncertainty out of Web browsing.

PC TIPS

Try an AOL free trial

If you'd like to try out AOL's online services to see if they suit you, you can take advantage of its free 30-day trial. UK residents need only telephone AOL on 0800 376 5432 and request a free copy of the software.

If you already have a connection to the Internet, you can visit AOL's Web site at www.aol.co.uk where you can download the installation software for free and find out how to use it. However, be warned: the installation software is over 10MB and it will take a long time to download to your computer. You might find it easier to order the CD-ROM by telephone. If you don't wish to continue using AOL after the trial period, simply telephone the company and cancel your account.

Connecting to AOL for the first time

There are many different types of Internet service provider and to connect requires a modem and access to a phone line. Here, we show you how to join AOL using one of their free 100-hour trial CD-ROMs.

1 Place the AOL CD-ROM in your CD-ROM drive. The program will start automatically. AOL recommends that no other programs (for example Word) are running during the installation, so shut down any open programs. The first screen you see asks whether you are joining as a new member or are just upgrading. Click on the New Members option.

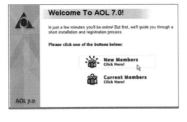

2 You will have to wait for a few moments while the software checks to see if any previous versions are installed on your hard disk. AOL automatically suggests a directory to install the software in, and it's best to accept the default and click on Next. The necessary files are now installed on your computer's hard disk from the CD-ROM. This may take a few minutes.

3 Once the file-copying process is complete, the AOL software searches for the modem. Make sure your modem is active, and also that Windows knows the modem is there (see pages 140–141). Click Next.

4 In the next screen the AOL software goes online and picks up the list of access numbers. First, make sure that United Kingdom is selected, then click Next. If you have voice-mail or touch-tone services, click on the appropriate options.

5 Click Next and AOL dials up to obtain a list of available numbers. A blue screen follows to show that AOL is trying to connect via your modem. You are now given a choice of numbers, depending on the AOL package you are installing. Follow the on-screen instructions to choose companies which provide your telephone services. Then click Next.

6 AOL displays your chosen numbers in a new window and asks you to confirm them again. Click on Next and AOL will try to connect to the Internet using the first number. If for some reason this is not available, it will try the next. Once connected to the AOL Internet site, the first screen will ask you if you want to create a new account. Select the top option and fill in the Registration Number and Password exactly as printed on the CD packaging. Then fill in the personal details on the next screen, and on the one after choose your payment method and fill in the details.

7 You are then asked to agree to AOL's Conditions of Service Agreement. Click on the I agree option to take you to the next series of screens that will allow you to finalize your AOL account details.

9 You're now a member, as you'll see from the AOL Welcome screen that appears, and the fact that email is awaiting your attention.

8 You now need to choose a screen name – the name you will use for email and by which you will be known online. Once you've done this, you also need to choose a personal password, which you confirm by typing it in twice. Then click Continue and AOL welcomes you to its services.

What you will find on AOL

You can start browsing the AOL channels and other services right away. Here we take a look at some of the most popular ones.

AOL is not accessible to all Internet users – it is a subscription service that only members can use. Designed with the new user and all ages in mind, the service is easily navigated by point and click operations, which are familiar to Windows users. You don't need to know any Web addresses or anything about search engines when you start; you can learn about these things at your own pace when you feel comfortable in the AOL areas. We've taken a look at seven of the most popular AOL channels on this page and the next.

LOCAL LIFE

The Local Life channel gives you the lowdown on what's happening all over the UK. Just click on the relevant area of the map and you'll get not just listings of what's on, but discussions and Chat rooms focusing on local issues, with topics ranging far and wide. Each area has its own selection of restaurants and hotels. You can see the average price of properties in your area, and look at street maps to get your bearings.

A number of major cities, including Manchester and Glasgow, get their own sub-channels within their respective regional sections, while London constitutes a region in itself.

NEWS

This is the place to find the latest news stories. There are links to the day's serious headline reports, as well as lighter 'news', and you also have the opportunity to discuss the topic of the day in the News Chat room. You can check out specialist sections for sport and business news, or focus on home news or international reports. There are eight main sections in addition to the banner headlines, plus you can also find out about the weather. Click on the Weather icon and this takes you to a new window with further options from which you can select the weather information you would like to view.

SPORT

The Sport channel supplies comprehensive coverage of just about every major sporting activity in separate sub-channels. You'll find features, results, match reports and more. There's also, of course, top-level latest news of the whole sporting world. There's plenty of interactive fun on offer as well, with a game of the week and sport trivia questions to tease your brain. You can also take part in the lively forums and discussions, and enter competitions to win tickets to top events. In fact, there's something for everyone.

ENTERTAINMENT

You can find a vast amount of show-business news and, of course, the all-important gossip on the channel devoted to the world of entertainment. There are main sections covering film, television and music. The TV section recommends essential viewing each day, while the Music

section has links allowing you to hear new releases, so you can enjoy a 'first listen'. The Film section provides news on the latest blockbusters and AOL Live gives you the chance to talk to celebrities via a Chat room. There are opportunities throughout to win competition prizes.

KIDS

The Kids channel is always packed with things to do. There's a resource of links to fun sites for youngsters on the Internet and a direct link to the Kids online Chat area. You can also play online games or take part in competitions to win lots of exciting goodies.

There is a more serious side to this AOL channel, with a Homework Help link for researching projects and topic revision exercises. All school ages are covered from primary through to A-level, and there's also an online dictionary to check spellings and meanings.

TECHNOLOGY

AOL's Technology Channel is densely packed with information and practical advice on just about every aspect of the computer world. You can buy software and hardware, check out software releases, download lots of useful programs – some of them free – and browse

highlights from the computer press. There's plenty of useful advice plus hints and tips for those who consider themselves beginners; if you don't find what you want here, then post a message in one of the many forums and the chances are that someone will come back with the answer you need.

CHAT & COMMUNITY

Every one of the AOL channels has a programme of hosted live-chat events throughout the week. The subjects covered are extremely varied. For instance, on one evening in the UK you could join online discussions about gardening, the paranormal, computing and kids' interests. You can view the schedule for the

week in advance by clicking on the Hosted Chat chat times link and, if nothing appeals, you can always enter some of the private chat areas, and raise any of your favourite topics until you find people who respond to your interests. If you're not sure how to get started, click on the New to Chat? to find out all about it.

An explanation of email

Wherever you and your PC are, you can send electronic mail, or email, to any other Internet user. You can also send and receive pictures, spreadsheets and other file types – almost instantly.

One of the most exciting aspects of connecting your computer to the Internet is the ability to send and receive electronic mail, or 'email'. Everywhere you look you see evidence of how popular email is – alongside telephone numbers and postal addresses for most businesses, there are now also email addresses. Email rivals the World Wide Web as the most popular use of the Internet. At its most basic, email is a fast way to send a written message to someone, but instead of using a pen and paper, typewriter or word processor, you use an email program on your computer to create and send messages.

The main advantages of email are its speed and flexibility: it is possible to send messages from your own PC to anyone in the world who has an email address, and vice versa, in minutes. And it is not only the written word that you can send. You can also dispatch pictures, programs and sound by email. This ability to send data electronically will save you postage or courier costs.

● The fax of life
When you send a fax, the recipient's machine could well be busy and you will have to tie up your phone line with repeated attempts to get through. In contrast, your email goes instantly via your Internet service provider (ISP) to the ISP of the person you want to contact.

You won't always receive an instant reply, however. Email won't be read until the recipient checks in to download their new messages. Therefore, the lightning speed of your email message zooming across the Internet is worthless if the person you are writing to only logs on to check for email once a week! However, most people who use email check for messages regularly and reply quickly.

For families and friends living in different countries, email is usually a cheaper and quicker option for sending messages and pictures than the post.

EMAIL IS CHEAP

The popularity of email is partly to do with its speed, but also its cost. Email can be cheap to use, particularly if you regularly keep in contact with family, friends or business colleagues abroad by telephone. An email is far cheaper than international telephone calls – even when you make the call during the cheap-rate times.

What's in an address?

Email addresses can look confusing at first. Here's a quick guide to the strange world of email addresses and how to read them.

A POSTAL ADDRESS includes a name, street, town, postcode and country. An email address contains different elements to this (see Understanding An Email Address, below). Most have a reference to the person's name, which may be spelt out in full or have an abbreviation of the person's first name or surname.

Next comes the @ symbol, pronounced 'at', followed by the name of the organization 'at' which the person is located.

This organization is usually an Internet service provider (ISP) or a company. It's also known as the domain and is where the recipient of the email has an account. The letters at the end of the domain indicate which type of organization manages the domain and often in which country the domain is based. For example, the letters '.co' show that the organization is a company, and '.uk' indicates that the organization is based in the United Kingdom.

● Naming names
When you decide to connect to the Internet you will have to choose a name to use as part of your email address. It's up to you what you select, but remember that your choice with any given ISP could well be limited by the number of other people who have joined. Every email address with an ISP has to be unique; you don't want email intended for you being sent to another person of the same name!

So, if your name is John Smith it is unlikely that you will be able to have 'johnsmith' as part of your email address. But what you can do is to add letters or numbers to make your name unique. Here we show examples

One advantage of email is that postal costs will be almost completely eliminated – reduced to the cost of a few seconds of a local telephone call.

of some of the variations that a person whose name is Mandy Hughes may either expect from, or suggest to, a fictional ISP called 'condor.co.uk'.

mhughes@condor.co.uk
mandy234@condor.co.uk
mandy.hughes@condor.co.uk
123456.1234@condor.co.uk

There are a few variations you may come across in email addresses. Instead of '.co', for example, you may see '.org' – this usually stands for a non-profit organization, such as a charity. Or you may see '.ac', which means 'academic' and refers to an educational institution, such as a university. No matter how a person's email address appears, as long as you enter it correctly into your email program (see next page) the recipient will get your message.

UNDERSTANDING AN EMAIL ADDRESS

1 The name of the person whose email account it is comes first. It may be a full name with the first and second name separated by a full stop (.), an abbreviation of the first name with the full surname or even a nickname.

2 The @ symbol separates the name of the person from the domain.

3 Next comes the domain name of the organization that stores the email messages for the recipient.

mhughes@condor.co.uk

4 Full stops separate the different elements that make up the domain. (There are never any spaces in an email address.)

5 The letters 'co' mean that the organization is a commercial company. (Most American companies have '.com' at the end of their domains.)

6 After the last full stop, 'uk' means that the organization is based in the United Kingdom.

WHAT IT MEANS
DOMAIN
This is jargon for an Internet site. Often, it's the name of a company, such as microsoft.com. Other times, it's the name of the Internet service provider with which the recipient has an account, such as aol.com.

Sending and receiving email

Outlook Express – now part of Windows XP and often supplied on ISP's CDs – is the most popular email program, and makes it easy to send and receive email messages.

IT'S EASY TO write a short email, click Send and make contact with a friend or relative. Here we show you how to communicate with people using your computer.

Windows XP includes Internet Explorer, software for browsing the World Wide Web, and Outlook Express, which allows you to send and receive email. We'll use Outlook Express to show you how to send and receive email, but since all email programs have similar features, you'll be able to apply the steps here to whichever program your ISP supplies, or that you decide to use.

Email software sorts your incoming and outgoing mail, clearly displaying whom your incoming mail is from and what it is about. There are also windows available that display a list of received and sent messages and where you can display and read the contents of your messages.

SITES TO @ VISIT

If you can't think of anyone to email, or aren't sure which of your friends or relatives have email accounts, your PC can help track them down if you're connected to the Internet.

There are several email directories which cover many countries of the world. You visit the Web site and type in the name of the person you're looking for, and the Web site will respond with a list of people that match the enquiry. Try these search sites to find long-lost friends:
www.whowhere.com
http://people.yahoo.com
www.bigfoot.com

1 To open Outlook Express, click on the Start button and select the Email option; it's near the top of the Start menu. You don't need to be connected to the Internet to write your messages. This helps to save on telephone call costs, as you only connect to transfer the messages.

2 The first time you start Outlook Express you'll receive a message straightaway from Microsoft, telling you about features of the program. This message appears in the top half of your Inbox screen. To read it, just highlight it with a single click and its contents will appear in the bottom half of the screen. The scroll bar on the right shows there is more to read. Click the scroll buttons to see more, just as you would in a word processor.

3 To reply to a message, click on the Reply button. This will create a reply window with the address of the person you are replying to already in place. All you have to do is enter the text of the message and click the Send button.

4 To send a new message, click on the Create Mail button. Enter the recipient's address in the To: line and a heading in the Subject: line. Type your message in the main area.

5 If you don't want to send the message straightaway, select Send Later from the File menu. A window appears telling you that the message will be placed in your Outbox ready to be sent when you choose.

6 When you are online and ready to send all your messages, click on the Send and Recv button. A dialog box will tell you the status of your outgoing and incoming mail. It's worth sending and receiving all your email in one go, as this will help you keep your telephone charges down.

7 You should check at regular intervals to see if you have received any email. Start Outlook Express and click the Send and Recv button. If you have new messages they will appear in your Inbox in the upper half of the screen. Just click on the message and it opens in the bottom half of the screen.

What happens when you send an email

Just as a letter goes from a post box to a sorting office and then on to the delivery address, an email follows an electronic route from your computer to an ISP, where it is 'sorted' and directed to the recipient's computer.

THE FIRST thing that happens to your message when you connect to your Internet service provider (ISP) to send your email, is that it's converted from the digital data that computers use, to analogue waves that telephone lines can cope with.

The initial stage of the journey takes the email from your end of the telephone line to the other end. This is the location of your ISP, where there are powerful computers known as mail servers. Rather like a normal postal sorting office, this is where the next stage of your email's journey is determined.

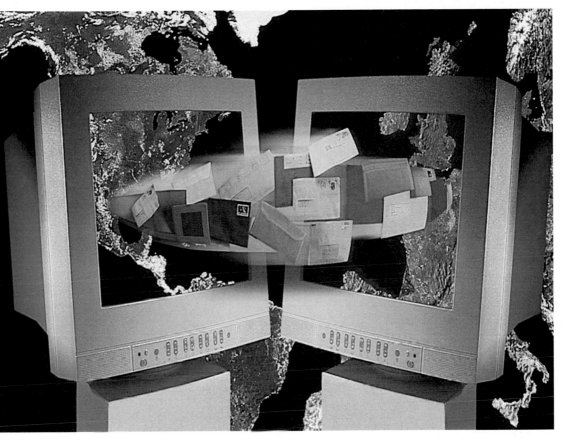

● Checking your email
The ISP's modem and computer converts the analogue waves from the telephone line back into digital information and looks at the address you are sending the mail to. It ensures that the mail was received correctly and then sends the message across the Internet to the recipient's ISP.

The recipient's ISP receives the mail and places it in a computer mail box, waiting for the recipient to dial up and collect, as they would with a PO Box. When the person you sent the message to dials their ISP, they're automatically notified that email is waiting for them. When they get their mail, their modem receives another analogue signal from the ISP's

Even if your email message is addressed to someone quite local to you, the path of the message might not only involve several different computers, but also different countries across the world.

computer. The modem converts this back to digital information and the email message appears – exactly as you sent it – on the screen of the recipient's computer.

EXPRESS YOURSELF WITH EMOTICONS

You might notice that some people include strange groups of characters in their email messages. Look at the messages from the side, and you'll see that they look like little faces. These are called emoticons – short for emotion icons.

Emoticons are used because it's hard to get a tone of voice – happy, sad, angry, etc – into a text-only email. To help them avoid misunderstandings, particularly when people didn't understand that a

comment was a joke, early computer users devised a shorthand way of being more expressive.

They used normal text characters to create icons. The first was a 'smiley', created by a colon, a dash and a right bracket. Together they look like this :-) which means 'I am feeling happy!'. Soon, other computer users came up with further variations using a range of characters, some of which are shown right.

:-(	I am sad
:-O	I am surprised
:-D	I am laughing
;-)	I am winking
8-)	I am wide-eyed or I am wearing spectacles
:-&	I am tongue-tied
>-(	I am angry
:-C	I don't believe it!
%-)	I've been staring at the screen too long!

Get more from email

Electronic mail is one of the great features of the Internet and you can do more with it than just send and receive messages. Here we show you what an extraordinary tool email can be.

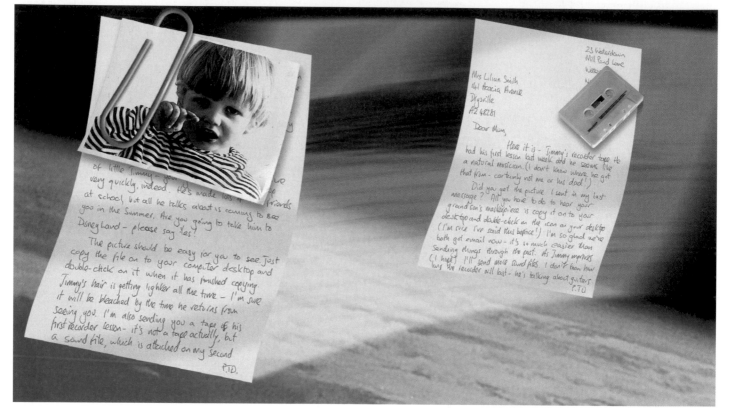

If you're already connected to the Internet, you have probably started using email in the same way that you would write a letter or send a fax. This one-to-one communication is the most common way of using email and lets you send messages across the world quickly and cheaply. However, although you're using email, you might not be taking advantage of its full range of powerful features.

● **Getting attached**
When you type in an email message and send it to a friend via the Internet, you are using the basic functions of email. One feature of email that you might find useful is to send an attachment with your message. An attachment is a file that is sent with the message – rather

Exciting possibilities open up when you learn how to attach files to your email messages.

like sending a letter with a parcel attached to it. The attachment can be any normal file, such as a Word document, Paint image or Excel spreadsheet. You can even send several files at a time. These files are transferred over the Internet to your friend or colleague, who will read your message and then open the file(s) attached to it. So, if you have to send reports to the office or just want to send a photograph to relatives living abroad, this is a fast and cheap way to move information around the world.

To attach a file to an email message just click on a paper clip icon, locate the file on your PC and press the Send button.

WATCH OUT FOR JUNK

Advertisers can buy lists of email addresses and send unwanted emails promoting a product or service – just like they do through your normal letterbox. These junk mail messages are not only intrusive, but you will have to pay for the time spent online and on the telephone while they download to your PC. Avoiding junk mail – or spam, as it's known to Internet users – is difficult. Even if there's a note at the bottom of the message about removing yourself from the spammer's list, this only tells the spammer that you read your mail. It's best to ignore all spam.

● **Automatic email**

So far, we have looked at the ways by which you can send a message to other people on the Internet (see pages 150–153). If they send a reply, you can read this with your email software. In effect, the system has worked in the same way as the post office delivers a letter. However, millions of people use email to keep up to date with news and features that cover a particular area of interest. This system is called a mailing list and there are tens of thousands of different mailing lists – covering just about every subject and hobby you can imagine.

To subscribe to a mailing list you need to send an email message to the computer that manages the list. Once you have subscribed, you will then receive any new information that is posted to the list. Any of the members of a list can post information that they think might be useful to other members. For example, if you want to learn Spanish, you might want to subscribe to a mailing list covering the Spanish language. The beauty of mailing lists is that once you have subscribed, the information arrives automatically on your computer and you can read it using your usual email software.

As there are thousands of different mailing lists and they are not usually publicized, you need to use a special database containing all the available lists. There are several of these 'lists of lists' on the Internet and one of the

(see pages 150–153)

PC TIPS

Research the list

A lot of the mailing lists are not meant for the general public, which means you should do a little research before joining. Topica, the directory site, tells you how to get more information before you join a group.

The reason for this is that, unlike Internet sites, lists are created and used by specific groups of people. The list Basset Hounds might well be a public group about dogs, but could just as easily be the name of a five-a-side football team in South Africa, or the joke name for a group of old school friends still keeping in touch via email.

Getting email without an email program

THE INCREASED availability of the Internet in libraries, Internet cafés, airports, colleges and other locations all over the world makes the possibility of being able to pick up your email from any computer with Internet access look like an extremely good idea. Some ISPs provide Web-based access to email – perfect when you are away from home. You can use any computer with Internet access: load your ISP's home page into the Web browser and follow the Webmail links. You'll need to know your user name and password and then you can send and receive messages. You use Web pages instead of an email program. If your ISP doesn't offer Web-based email, you can sign up with a site which specializes in it, such as Hotmail (see p157).

Energis Ision is an example of an ISP offering webmail. From any computer, a subscriber can access the Ision site and click on Webmail to see what messages are waiting there. Messages can be read, deleted or left for retrieval at the 'home' PC later.

most popular is called Topica (formerly known as Liszt) – it's found at www.liszt.com. It contains details of 90,000 mailing lists on the Internet and lets you search through the database for a list that covers your areas of interest. Once you have selected a list that sounds suitable, it tells you how to subscribe to it or discover more about the list.

● **Subscribing to a list**

Subscribing to a mailing list is easy – you send an email with a key phrase (Topica helps you find this) to the manager of the mailing list, which then adds you to it. Each mailing list has a different key phrase, so read the subscription instructions carefully.

When you send your email asking to subscribe, you'll normally address it to the 'majordomo'. This is a program that reads your email and, if it detects the key phrase, will automatically add you to the list.

The Topica site (www.liszt.com) is a comprehensive directory of over 90,000 mailing lists. It works like a search engine as you type in a search query. Always check the nature of the mailing list before you join (see PC Tips).

Adding an attachment to an email message

Email is a great way to send files around the world easily and cheaply. Here's your guide to attaching a photograph to a message – and the method is the same when sending other file types.

1 Launch your email program using the Start button. Here we are using Netscape Messenger, supplied as part of the Netscape Communicator suite and of which the browser Navigator is a part, but other email programs work in a similar way. When Netscape Messenger has loaded, click on the New Msg button in the toolbar (inset).

2 Clicking on the New Msg button opens a new, blank email document.

3 Enter the email address in the To: box. In this example we are sending a message to a relative in Australia. Move your cursor to the Subject: box and click to type in a description of the message.

4 Now we're ready to enter the main message. Email is great for a short note like this – updating a relative on the latest family developments. We are going to attach a photograph to the message, so when we've finished typing, we click on the paper clip Attach button on the toolbar.

5 Hold down the mouse button on the Attach button and then click on File from the drop-down menu that appears. The Enter File to attach window appears. We're looking for a picture that is in the My Pictures folder, which is within the My Documents folder. Double-click on the My Pictures folder to open it and then double-click on the picture you want.

6 Double-clicking on the picture automatically attaches the picture to our message, which appears as an icon in the panel above the Subject: box. Once you have connected to your Internet service provider, click on the Send button on the toolbar and your message will be sent, complete with the attached photograph.

CHECKPOINT ✔

ATTACHING FILES

☑ Be wary of using file names over eight letters as not all computers recognize long file names.

☑ Make it obvious which version of a program you're using. For example, if you send a spreadsheet to someone with Excel version 5 and you have Excel version 7, you need to save the file in version 5 format, or it may not work when the recipient tries to open it.

☑ It's not always a good idea to attach large files (over 1MB) to email messages due to the time and expense spent online when sending them.

Sign up with Hotmail

You might want the flexibility to change your ISP, but you don't want to constantly change your email address. One option is to use a Hotmail address, then your friends will always be able to reach you and you'll be able to check your mail wherever you are by logging onto the Hotmail site.

1 Start your Internet browser and connect to the Hotmail site at www.hotmail.com. Click on the Sign Up link at the top of the page (inset).

2 On the next screen that appears, there are two sections that you need to fill in. The first is your profile information, which requires your basic details.

3 In the second section of your registration form you need to fill in your new hotmail account information. This includes your email address, and you will need to select and type in a password. Repeat it for confirmation. Choose something that you can remember but that nobody else is likely to guess.

4 At the bottom of this page is a box detailing the terms and conditions of the Hotmail service. Once you have read through this agreement between yourself and Microsoft Corporation you have the option of clicking I Agree to proceed, or click Cancel to discontinue your registration.

5 The next screen shows that your registration is complete and confirms your new email address. Click the Continue button to proceed to the next page.

6 The final screen offers you the chance to upgrade your account for a fee of £19.99 per year. This includes more storage and the ability to send and receive large attachments. If you wish to proceed with the upgrade, click Continue to Billing Information. Otherwise, go to the Click here link (inset).

7 Even if you don't upgrade, the next couple of screens display free subscriptions and MSN featured offers. Click on Continue, then Continue to E-mail to get to the home page of your Hotmail account. This is the page that will now appear whenever you log on to your hotmail account after connecting to the site.

DON'T FORGET TO LOG IN

With a standard 2MB Hotmail account you must log in every 30 days to keep your account active. However, if you upgrade to a 10MB hotmail account, your account will remain active regardless of whether or not you sign in, as long as your subscription is valid.

● Acknowledgments

Abbreviations: t = top; b = bottom; r = right;
l = left; c = centre.
All cartoons are by Chris Bramley

8 De Agostini
11tr De Agostini
12 Dave Jordan/De Agostini
16 Steve Bartholomew/De Agostini
18t Steve Bartholomew/De Agostini
20 br N Lloyd/De Agostini; tl De Agostini
21tr N Lloyd/De Agostini
22 De Agostini
24 Steve Bartholomew/De Agostini
25 tl Image Bank; b De Agostini
27tl Steve Bartholomew/De Agostini
32 De Agostini
34tr De Agostini
35br De Agostini
36 Dave Jordan/De Agostini
38 De Agostini
42 Gettyone Stone
46tr Steve Bartholomew/De Agostini
    (background: Image Bank)
    bl Steve Bartholomew/De Agostini
49 Steve Bartholomew/De Agostini
50 De Agostini
53l Dave Jordan/De Agostini
54 De Agostini
56 Steve Bartholomew/De Agostini
58 De Agostini
60 De Agostini
61tl De Agostini

62b Gettyone Stone
63b Steve Bartholomew/De Agostini
64 De Agostini
66 Steve Bartholomew/De Agostini
68 De Agostini
70 De Agostini
72t Steve Bartholomew/De Agostini
74 De Agostini
76br Steve Bartholomew/De Agostini
78 De Agostini
80 Gettyone Stone
82 De Agostini
84 Steve Bartholomew/De Agostini
85tl Steve Bartholomew/De Agostini
86 De Agostini
87tl De Agostini
90 t Sony; tr VideoLogic; c & br Hewlett-
    Packard; bl Microsoft Corporation
91 tl Epson (UK) Ltd; tr Hewlett-Packard;
    cl SONICblue; cr Eastman Kodak
    Company; br Microsoft Corporation;
    bl & bc De Agostini
92 tl Hewlett-Packard; tc Intel Corporation
    (UK) Ltd; cl Creative Labs (UK) Ltd;
    br Creative Labs (UK) Ltd; tr, c & cr
    De Agostini
93 De Agostini
94 Dave Jordan/De Agostini
95 t Gettyone Stone; c Steve
    Bartholomew/De Agostini; b Science &
    Society Picture Library, London
96 Storm/De Agostini
97 Storm/De Agostini

98 De Agostini
100 Steve Bartholomew/De Agostini
101(all) De Agostini
102 b Epson (UK) Ltd; tr & c De Agostini
103 l Samsung Electronics (UK) Ltd;
    c Hewlett-Packard
104 Hewlett-Packard/De Agostini
107 Storm/De Agostini
110 De Agostini
112l Bridgeman Art Library, London; tr, cr &
    br Telegraph Colour Library, London;
    bc De Agostini
114 De Agostini
116 Steve Bartholomew/De Agostini
120 De Agostini
122 De Agostini
123 De Agostini
124 De Agostini
125 De Agostini
126 Allsport
128 Image Bank
132 tl & cr Gettyone Stone; tc TRIP;
    c De Agostini
136t Dave Jordan/De Agostini; br TRIP
138 Robotics
140t Steve Bartholomew/De Agostini,
    b Global Village
150t Image Bank, b De Agostini
151t Image Bank
153 Image Bank
154 De Agostini (background NASA)